THE STORY OF
DICTATORSHIP

THE STORY OF DICTATORSHIP

FROM THE EARLIEST TIMES TILL TO-DAY

" Ausi omnes immane nefas, ausoque potiti "

by
E. E. KELLETT, M.A.

*Formerly Scholar of Wadham College, Oxford,
and University Prizeman;
author of "Short History of Religions,"
"Fashion in Literature,"
"Short History of the Jews," etc.*

1937
E. P. DUTTON AND COMPANY, INC.
PUBLISHERS   NEW YORK

COPYRIGHT, 1937, BY
E. P. DUTTON & CO., INC.
ALL RIGHTS RESERVED
PRINTED IN THE U.S.A.

First Edition

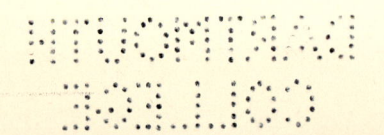

CONTENTS

	PAGE
INTRODUCTION	7
A HEBREW TYRANT	23
THE GREEK TYRANNIES	34
SICILY	52
RENAISSANCE ITALY	78
NAPOLEON	100
SOUTH AMERICA	111
MODERN TYRANNIES:	
RUSSIA	131
ITALY	143
GERMANY	168
AUSTRIA	187
CONCLUSION	200
APPENDIX	221
INDEX	223

INTRODUCTION

"Nihil sub sole novum; nec valet quisquam dicere, Ecce hoc recens est."—*Ecclesiastes*.

THERE are certain times in human history which appear to be favourable to the rise of men whom the ancient Greeks called Tyrants. Political difficulties of various kinds—the sense that the established government was incompetent or corrupt, the troubles following a war, the necessity, during a war, of entrusting the command to a single hand, mere ennui or discontent, which the people might be unable to explain to themselves—these, or some of these, have provided the opportunity for a man of energy and daring to raise himself above the laws. Or it may be that social changes, the causes or effects of political disturbances, have lain at the root of these occurrences. It is plausibly maintained, for example, that the growth of trade, and its advance in certain unforeseen directions, were a main cause of the discontent with the rule of Charles I. The discontent led to civil war; the civil war destroyed the established dynasty; and hence the Protectorate of Oliver Cromwell, which was grudgingly accepted by the people in preference to utter anarchy. The immense increase of commerce—immense relatively to the area affected—in the Greek world about six hundred years before Christ, has been similarly assigned as the explanation of the appearance of tyrannies, almost simultaneously, in scores of Greek cities. The old systems of government were bewildered by the phenomenon, and did not know how to deal with it. Rich money-lenders oppressed their debtors, the poor groaned under the oppression, a " deliverer " appeared, and ere long the cities saw what France saw under the Second Empire—an equality of all, high or low, under the domination of a splendid court. We have seen, in plentiful measure, things of this kind in our own days.

The historians and philosophers of Rome and Greece were, as we might expect, keenly interested in these phenomena, and have given us their opinions upon them. They studied the tyrants individually, and compared them with one another, discussing their rise, their glory, and their fall ; and the conclusions reached are very remarkable. For, while recognising their ability, and making allowance for the circumstances which conditioned their appearance, the philosophers and historians are all but unanimous in their condemnation. The tyrants, they admit, were not always tyrannical in our sense of the word ; some of them ruled mildly, some were, so far as we can judge, popular with the mass of the citizens ; many raised their country to a height of glory and power which it never reached under other forms of government. But the fact remained that they made *themselves* rulers, that they showed no intention of laying down their power when the people so desired, and that their own will was the law.

" Sic volo, sic jubeo, sit pro ratione voluntas." Hence, when statists discussed forms of government, they either, like Aristotle, quietly assumed that tyranny was the worst of all, or if, like Cicero, they were rhetorically inclined, broke out into loud and vigorous denunciation. "Than the tyrant," says Cicero, "no animal more hateful can be conceived, or more justly detested, alike by gods and by men; he wears indeed a human shape, but in character is worse than the most savage beasts." And it is noteworthy that these judgments are not those of democrats. Aristotle was no partisan of the Athenian system, and indeed was more comfortable in Macedon or under the tyrant Hermeias than with the Athenian assemblies. Plato frankly hated the constitution of his native city, and once, unfortunately for himself, tried to make friends with a tyrant. Cicero, dubiously and hesitatingly, supported the Roman oligarchy. Yet all alike preferred any system short of anarchy to despotism, and carried to the utmost lengths their hatred of the despot.

Here, if nowhere else, the populace agreed with the "highbrow." One had only to accuse a man of aiming at a tyranny to rouse the common people against him. Killing such a man was no murder;* of all Athenians none were more highly honoured than Harmodius and Aristogeiton, who were fancied, quite mistakenly, to have delivered the city from its tyrants; and of all Corinthians the most glorious was Timoleon, who killed his own brother for merely aiming at a tyranny. It was said that the rarest of sights was a grey-haired tyrant; and the man

---

* The same view was passionately maintained in the nineteenth century by Mazzini, who yet declared that, so soon as any country was free, capital punishment ought to be abolished. The tyrant is an outlaw; between him and the oppressed citizen there is an eternal war, and it is no worse to kill him in the street than to shoot him in battle. Or rather it is nobler; for you kill a single guilty man, and not, as in war, a thousand innocents. "In face of the tyrant rises the tyrannicide."

who had shortened the life of such an " animal " was a public benefactor. Those who had suffered under him consoled themselves by drawing lurid pictures of the state of his mind. He endured, so they imagined, all the tortures of the damned. " He is," says Plato, " a prisoner hemmed in by a ring of warders, all of them his enemies; he is full of multitudinous terrors and longings of every kind. Though of a greedy and inquisitive disposition, he is the only man in the city who cannot set his eyes on those things which everyone desires to see; he buries himself in his house, and is consumed with envy of those who dare to go abroad; he is the most abject of slaves, compelled to flatter and bribe the worst of men; he thinks himself rich and is in truth a pauper. Nor can he hope to mend; by the necessity of his position he must become more and more envious, faithless, impure, and friendless, the host and nurse of ever-deepening vice." We might almost be reading the words of Eliphaz: " The wicked man travaileth with pain all his days, even the number of years that are laid up for the oppressor: a sound of terrors is in his ears; in prosperity the spoiler shall come upon him. He believeth not that he shall return out of darkness, and he is waited for of the sword. Distress and anguish make him afraid; they prevail against him as a king ready for the battle." It was of these men that Tacitus was thinking when he moralised upon the terrible words of Tiberius' letter to the Senate, " What to write to you, Conscript Fathers, or how to write, or what not to write, may the gods and goddesses confound me worse than I daily feel myself confounded, if I know." " Not for nothing," says Tacitus, " does the wise philosopher declare that, could the hearts of tyrants lie open before us, we should see there the most horrible wounds and ulcers; for the mind is lacerated with cruelty and lust as hideously as the body with blows."

There is a curious chapter in Herodotus which has attracted wide attention. Seven Persian nobles, he tells us, were conspiring against the Magian usurper of the throne. They met together to discuss their plans. At this meeting, says the historian, speeches were made, though many Greeks deny the fact. Certain it is that the speeches, as reported, are more Greek than Persian; but they are none the less interesting. That of Otanes, in particular, reveals the Greek view of monarchy. "The rule of one," says Otanes, "is neither good nor pleasant. Ye cannot have forgotten to what lengths Cambyses went in his haughty tyranny, and the haughtiness of the Magians ye have yourselves experienced. How indeed is it possible that monarchy should be well adjusted, when it allows a man to do as he likes without having to answer for it? Such license cannot but rouse strange ideas even in the heart of the best of men. Give a man this power, and forthwith his many good things exalt him with pride; and envy, which in any case is natural to man, unavoidably arises within him. But in pride and envy are included all wickedness, either of them driving him on to violent and savage deeds. True, one might expect that kings, having all that heart can wish, ought to be free from envy; but the opposite is seen to be the case. They are jealous of the most virtuous among their subjects, and desire their death; while those whom they most delight in are the vilest and worst, for they have always an open ear for slanderers and lying tales. Nor can a king be constant and of one mind. Pay him moderate respect, and he is angry because your respect is insufficient; give him profound homage, and he is again offended, because, as he says, you spaniel him at heels. But, worst of all, he disregards the laws of the country, puts men to death without trial and violates women."

This feeling prevailed not merely when a single man was the tyrant, but when a nation became tyrannical. Whether such a nation ruled mildly or violently made little difference. The Athenian Empire, for example, was certainly, for the times in which it existed, a very moderate despotism. But it was denounced by its enemies as a "tyranny", and the Athenians themselves did not repudiate the name. Not merely the rash and noisy Cleon, but the refined and cautious Pericles, owned that their rule over their subjects was precisely what that of Peisistratus had been over themselves. It began in the well-known fashion. Athens offered herself as the deliverer of the islands from the Persians, and then gradually asserted her own dominion; taxed them for her own good, and used the tribute for the adornment of herself. She was determined not to resign the position she had gained. "It came to us almost by accident," said Pericles, "but it would be dangerous to give it up." Athens, in fact, had played the part which the fable of Stesichorus assigned to the man. The horse, wishing to overcome the stag, allowed the man to mount him. The stag was indeed overcome, but the man has been on horseback ever since. This fable expresses exactly the methods of the would-be tyrant; and it is a summary of the history of Athenian rule. It was a plausible contention that the rule was to the advantage of the subject cities : and certainly Persia was a more cruel mistress than Athens ever was ; but, in spite of everything that could be said, the rule was hated : and the Spartans, when the Peloponnesian War began, gained numberless allies by playing on the feeling. And the feeling was even stronger against the individual tyrant.

If such was the case ; if uncontrolled power is so hateful ; if the tyrant inevitably degenerates ; and if he must know that his subjects, and even those in no danger of subjection, hold this view of him, one might imagine that a tyranny is the very last thing to which a man would aspire. A position which necessarily makes him envious is hardly likely to be enviable. Nevertheless, such is the glamour of power, that men are constantly found who, when the opportunity arises, are ready to seize dominion, and even to fancy themselves in a sense happy when they have attained it. "Mother," says Eteocles in the Phœnissæ of Euripides :

> "Mother, I will not hide my thoughts from thee,
> I'd scale the farthest dwellings of the stars,
> Or seek the lowest depths beneath the earth,
> To gain that greatest goddess, Tyranny."

This is a feeling which we all harbour at times. What advocate of one man one vote does not occasionally wish that he had a million votes himself, in order to carry through a favourite policy of his own ? Even Cicero, when aflame with indignation against what he regarded as the tyranny of Julius Cæsar, naïvely confesses that he has had the desire to be a tyrant himself—though he is careful to add that he would rather die a thousand times than seriously cherish the idea. Others are less scrupulous. So early as the time of the Judges, as we shall see, we find the bramble far from unwilling to lord it over the cedars of Lebanon. At a later date in Greece, when a combination of circumstances favoured the despotic impulse, the country swarmed with tyrants, who, by variations of very similar devices, made themselves masters of Sicyon, Argos, Corinth, Athens, Syracuse, Agrigentum. When, about the time of the Renaissance, Italy was in much the same condition, the small independent republics were everywhere displaced by tyrannies: the Medici in Florence, the Visconti and Sforza in Milan, the Este in Ferrara, all did, *mutatis mutandis*, as Dionysius and Peisistratus had done two thousand years before them. In a distant century, and in lands undreamt of by Phalaris, the Francias and Lopezes followed, without knowing it, the example of Phalaris: they took their chances, slaughtered their enemies, distrusted their closest friends; and they in their turn have imitators to-day. On a more conspicuous stage, the Lenins, Hitlers, Pilsudskis, Kemals, Mussolinis are plying the old trade. They have utilised the post-war troubles, much as Sulla used the chaos which followed the civil wars of Rome, to raise themselves above their fellows. None of these men is an original. Allowance being made for mechanical and social changes, their methods of gaining and keeping power are practically the same as those adopted by their Sicilian or Italian prototypes. They may have been financiers, professing to put right a monetary crisis. So, as far as we can see, was Pheidon of Argos. They may have been demagogues, protectors of the poor against the rich. So was Dionysius. They may have been soldiers, turning the armies of the State against the State. Such were scores of their predecessors. All their devices, for retaining their place, the suppression of public opinion, the invention of bugbears and scapegoats, the deliberate cultivation of national hatreds in the name of patriotism, the " busying of giddy minds with foreign quarrels "—every one of these is a mimicry of a trick practised, it may be on a smaller scale, two thousand years since, and probably two thousand years before that.* There is but one new thing about it all—a novel and sounding name. Tyranny is called National Socialism, or disguised as the Totalitarian State. But even this is not really new. The ancient tyrants recognised as clearly as the modern the advantage of using euphemisms— pleasant names for unpleasant things, though they did not hit on phrases quite so imposing.

Most of these men, in the present day, are known as Dictators—an unlucky misnomer. For the Roman dictator was a constitutional officer, legally appointed, to meet a special emergency, and for six months only.† Repeatedly, if the emergency was successfully met, he

* There are traces of similar things in China millenniums ago, and we see the same processes in China to-day.

† Such an officer was called by the Greeks an Æsymnete. We find examples of Æsymnetes who used their powers to turn themselves into tyrants. But there is one very conspicuous exception. In a very dangerous crisis, the people of Mitylene elected Pittacus, one of the " Seven Wise Men," their Æsymnete, for the very long term of ten years, during which he was to have absolute power. At the end of the period, having accomplished his task, Pittacus resigned, and went back into private life. There were people who were as greatly astonished at his action as was Napoleon at the fact that Wellington, after Waterloo, made no attempt to turn George III off the throne.

resigned before the end of his term, and fell back into the ranks of the ordinary citizens. But the essence of the modern "dictatorship" is precisely the opposite. Like the ancient tyrant, he means his office to be permanent. Even Sulla, the calmest and most murderous of all Roman Dictators, was, at least in show, legally chosen, and, when he conceived the emergency to have been duly met, dismissed his lictors, abdicated all his functions, and retired to his villa at Puteoli to pursue his sensual or refined pleasures. But his modern imitator suits rather the definition given by a Roman historian: "Those men are called *tyranni* who retain a permanent power in states which before have enjoyed liberty." I make no apology, therefore, for calling them by their proper name, and for marking the likenesses between them and their true progenitors. There is no similarity between a Mussolini and a Fabius Cunetator; nor would Cincinnatus recognise his dictatorial office in the monarchical sway of a Pilsudski: but there *is* a similarity between Franco and Agathocles.

True, the use of modern machinery tends to conceal from us the essential likeness between the tyrants of to-day and those of old. Hitler and Mussolini, by borrowing the latest devices of advertisers, or by availing themselves of the achievements of applied science, have been able to gain for themselves a popularity which it would be ridiculous to deny. Every possible form of propaganda has been skilfully utilised; the wireless has been pressed into the service; the newspapers, which had been supposed to be the safety-valves of discontent and the chief defenders of freedom, are controlled and compelled to speak with one voice ;* the schools are regimented and the schoolmaster thoroughly disciplined in his task of teaching the young idea almost literally how to shoot ; the charms of music are used to soothe uneasy feelings or to stir the heroes to arm for battle ; a cult of the Führer or of the Duce is preached as the sole orthodoxy of the nation ; and the people have gradually been trained to think nothing but what the Government wishes them to think. Hence we find that whole populations are totally unconscious of their slavery, and will stoutly deny that they are in chains. None of these powerful engines, mental or physical, were known to a Peisistratus ; and we are inclined to smile at the crudity of the methods which he was driven to employ : in fact, we can scarcely see that, in essence, they were exactly the same as those now so common. When Peisistratus had been expelled from Athens, and desired to return, he and his partisans dressed up a tall and beautiful woman to represent Athene, surrounded her with all the usual attendants of the goddess, and drove with her into the city, while heralds proclaimed aloud that it was the divine will that the ruler should be restored. This is not the kind of stratagem a modern tyrant would adopt ; but, for its time and place, it was as well suited as the aeroplanes, fanfares, or army-manœuvres with which Hitler reinforces his appeals. But naturally it could not, in the long-run, be quite as effective. It was to modern devices what the Rocket was to the latest Flying Scotsman. There was always an opposition which could not quite be silenced,

---

* De Bono, in Abyssinia, found foreign journalists " undisciplined ", and turned them out. Italian journalists, being " disciplined ", were retained.

and the curses, if not loud, were deep. Nowadays, there are few who even wish to curse. The play of subtle forces, visible or invisible, long-continued and persistent, has made men as loyal to these rulers as the Cavaliers were to the Stuarts or Dr. Johnson to George III.

In all ages men have worshipped success. There were, in Greece, plenty of people to extol, to flatter, and to envy the tyrant who had once established himself. But it is doubtful if there was ever a time when success was so openly worshipped as now. Hence these same tyrants, who would have been utterly despised had they failed—nay, who actually *were* despised while they seemed likely to fail—find admirers in countries not their own, and are vociferously belauded by men who would be the first to suffer were the despotic system introduced in their own nation. Newspaper proprietors vie with each other in eulogising rulers who would no sooner obtain power than they would send the eulogists to concentration camps; and men whose governments allow them freedom of speech use that freedom to panegyrise men whose first principle is not to allow it. This stands in painful contrast to the vigour with which ancient writers, wherever they were at liberty to do so, denounced the tyrant and his tyranny.

There was another point of difference between the old times and the new. In the Greek world, quarrelsome as it was, there was a curious underlying sense of unity. Those tiny States, jealous of their independence as they were, were yet a comity, and harboured an Hellenic conscience. Rarely, indeed, for instance, did they make slaves of Greek captives, whatever they might do with barbarians. When such a thing was done a thrill of horror ran through the whole Greek world. In slighter, but by no means negligible, measure, the national conscience seems to have been shocked by tyrants and tyrannies, even though the tyrants might be mild and the tyrannies endurable. Thus, when the leading state of Sparta put the despots down, there seems to have been a widespread feeling of relief, and a general approval of her action.

Such a thing is impossible to-day. There is, in spite of the terrible dissensions, a European sentiment, and amid all the discords, a European concert, and this has, in the past, led nations to interfere in order to put an end to oppression in one or other member of the family. But such endeavours were rarely successful, and we are now almost universally convinced that interference in the internal affairs of individual countries is to be ruled out. Fascism is, we may hope, not likely to prevail in England or France; but England and France leave Fascism to work its will in Italy: and Fascism itself has done at least lip-service to the principle in regard to the affairs of Spain. Even Bolshevism, which at one time was an aggressive and propagandist religion, aiming at universal conquest, has more or less consented to confine its energies within its own boundaries.

Thus, on the whole, the present attitude towards dictatorships tends to be one of toleration. Millions of free men feel, as strongly as ever, that they would prefer death to submission to " dictatorial " domination. But they say that, if other peoples prefer such submission, they must be left to submit. If Germans worship Hitler, that is a German affair. And toleration not infrequently merges in a kind of approval, of which there are signs even in England to-day.

Thus there is neither a consensus, more or less complete, of detestation of tyranny, nor any power, like Sparta, capable of putting it down. Europe, at the present moment, is dividing into two parties, the differences between which are irreconcilable : the one regarding the individual as nothing and the State as everything, the other proclaiming that the State exists for the good of the individual. In ancient Greece there might be differences of race—Dorian or Ionian—or differences between oligarchies and democracies, but it was everywhere held that tyrannies were un-Greek excrescences, fit perhaps for barbarians, but degrading to the Hellene. A Spartan, though the discipline to which he submitted himself was severe almost beyond parallel, prided himself that his city had never known a tyrant ; Athens felt shame that she had once been under a tyranny, and was determined never again to incur the disgrace. To-day things are not so.

Nevertheless, the truth must be spoken. The Dictator remains a tyrant, the Totalitarian State is a prison, and its subjects are closed in by walls none the less real because they are invisible to the captives. Despite superficial differences, there *are* likenesses, and very profound ones, between the present-day rulers and the Greek or Italian despots. The Phalaris of to-day has no Brazen Bull, but he has his Lipari Islands or his concentration camps ; and it cannot be useless to study, however briefly, the modern despots alongside the ancient. I might have written in Plutarchian fashion, a series of Parallel Lives, each pair followed by an essay entitled " Dionysius and Hitler Compared," or " Pheidon and Salazar Contrasted." But such disquisitions are unnecessary ; the history will carry its own moral, and I prefer to leave the reader to draw such comparisons, pleasant or odious, for himself.

It is, of course, impossible to describe, even in the merest outline, a tithe of the tyrannies which have arisen in the world at various times. I must content myself with a few typical examples ; and I will begin with one which seems to me of special interest in that, though it is the earliest of which we have any account, it exhibits, in remarkable fashion, many of the characteristic features of the *genre*.

A HEBREW TYRANT

"Abimelech made his government a tyranny, and constituted himself a lord, to do what he pleased in disregard of the laws; and as for those who were advocates of justice, against them he acted more harshly than against any others."—*Josephus*.

THE history of Israel differs from that of Greece or Rome in being Oriental. It exhibits plenty of tyrannies, and of course, as Easterners are human, and love of power is a universal failing, the Hebrew tyrants are easily recognised as belonging to the same class as a Dionysius or a Sulla; but in some respects they show the tyrannic qualities in an exaggerated form. Their dynasties, for example, are short-lived after the manner so familiar in the history of India. An energetic soldier makes himself ruler, and generally contrives to pass on his dominion to his son. The son is less able and energetic. The grandson—if he succeeds at all—is nearly always a degenerate, who is deposed by another energetic soldier; and the cycle begins again. We think of Jeroboam and Nadab, Baasha and Elah, Omri, Ahab, and Jehoram. It is like the proverbial course of our merchant princes, poor, wealthy, and then poor again.

This circular tour is of course what we find with the Greek tyrant-dynasties, though there the descent is often less sudden. The Hellenic character is perhaps not so prone to luxury and debauchery as the Oriental; and it was necessary for the Western despot to pay more attention to public opinion than for a ruler to do so in lands which had from time immemorial been accustomed either to sultanates or to the unquestioned authority of sheikhs. But there were other features which conditioned a more marked and important distinction. The Eastern monarchies were not built up on the city-state: their units were areas of comparatively great size; and this in itself is enough to mark them off from the Hellenic types. A kingship was already there, established as the recognised form of government; and all that a Jehu had to do, after murdering every member of the family he was displacing, was to assume the kingly title, and the prestige of kingship became his almost immediately. Such a man did indeed use, so far as the conditions allowed, the devices which every aspiring despot must use: like Jeroboam he would pose as the friend of the poor, or as the saviour of his country from foreign enemies; and he would strengthen his position by nationalising the religion, by setting up a Golden Calf at Bethel that the people might not go up to Jerusalem to worship; but this once done, the mere name of king was sufficient to lend him a touch of legitimacy, and in a very short time he who had been a traitor to his own king was able to treat a revolt against himself as treason.*

Doubtless, if we knew the internal history of the little cities which Israel conquered, Jericho, Ai, Debir, we might find that many of the rulers who are called " kings " by the historian were really " tyrants " in something

---

* So Richard III, when once crowned, could say:

"Besides, the king's name is a tower of strength,
Which they upon the adverse party want."

like the Greek sense; but when once a more or less ordered kingdom had been established, the more precise title would seem to be "usurpers." Athaliah, for instance, was a queen-usurper; and it is clear that the partisans of Saul regarded David in a similar light, and spoke of him with the horror with which, as we have seen, Cicero speaks of the Sullas and Mariuses. But even to Shimei David was a king.

Nevertheless, despite these differences, there is in Biblical history one story of a man whom the Greeks themselves might have called a "tyrannus", and whose whole conduct is remarkably parallel to that of a Dionysius or an Agathocles. Unless some of the early Egyptian rulers were of this character, the narrative records the very earliest tyranny of which we have record.

The tale, which is told all too briefly and obscurely, is to be found in the Book of Judges. Obscure as it is, however, the reader will, I think find it very illuminating. This barbarous half-Canaanite tyrant shows a precocious skill in the application of methods adopted, much later, by men of whom I shall have to speak in the following chapters; and the teller of the story expresses, in his own peculiar theological language, the same detestation of the tyrant's crimes which Plato and other philosophers show, in their own dialects, towards the villainies of the despots whose acquaintance they had so painfully made.

Gideon, a Manassite chieftain of a city called Ophrah, had gained great prestige by rescuing his people from the ravages of certain Bedouin tribes, whose perpetual raids had been as destructive as the visitations of clouds of locusts. Not unnaturally, his authority, though loose and undefined in a society not yet knit together, was great throughout a wide region; but he made no attempt —indeed he openly refused—to stretch it beyond what was then regarded as due and proper. To use a modern term, he kept within constitutional limits; the other chiefs retained their rank and position, and exercised their patriarchal functions as before. As the years went by, we may imagine that his counsels were listened to with the sort of respect which the Greek leaders before Troy paid to Nestor: and this authority remained with him till his death. People remembered that, in the first glow of gratitude for the deliverance he had given, a kind of kingship had been offered him, and he had rejected it: they therefore followed his counsels much more willingly than they would have obeyed his regal commands.

Like other great sheikhs, Gideon had a large harem, and we are told that he had no fewer than seventy legitimate sons, who, though of course not succeeding to his full prestige, would be able to build upon it, and form a sort of aristocracy, much as, in some Greek and Italian cities, it was rather the family that ruled than a single member of it. But there was one son who had different ideas.

In the disjointed confederacy which Gideon had saved and afterwards protected, was the mainly Canaanite city of Shechem. One of Gideon's wives was a Canaanite woman of this city, and her son was Abimelech, a name ever afterwards remembered in Palestine. Abimelech was a man of ruthless energy: like Edmund, he made

Nature his goddess, and bound his services to her law. Doubtless his inferior birth rankled in his mind, and he may have been embittered by some contemptuous treatment which he had received from his more fortunate brothers. At any rate no sooner was his father dead than he formed his plans. He went at once to Shechem, where his mother's kinsmen seem to have been the dominant oligarchy. "Which is better for you," he said, "that seventy men rule over you, or that one man rule over you?" As in any case they would be more or less subject to Ophrah, it was better that they should be subject to one man rather than to a mob. "The rule of many is not good," said Odysseus to the Greeks at Troy; "let there be one captain, one king." The argument was a strong one, and it was supported by another: "Remember that I am your bone and your flesh." The townsmen recognised the bond; they said "He is our brother"; and their hearts turned to Abimelech.

It is a sagacious remark of Thucydides that tyrannies did not arise in Greece until money began to flow into the country: and it is a significant fact that one of the earliest of the tyrants, Pheidon of Argos, was also the first Greek to invent a coinage. There are some scholars, indeed, as we shall see, who would explain the rise of the tyrants by pointing to the recent appearance of coined money, which the would-be tyrant contrived to seize. At any rate, every tyrant felt the need of money; and the first step of Abimelech was to secure it. As usual in ancient times the temple was the bank; and to the temple his kinsmen gave him access. He took seventy shekels, a shekel for the life of each of his brothers, and with this sum hired a "list of lawless resolutes"—men described in the original by the term "Raca", which as we know survived till the time of Christ as a word denoting the extreme of villainy. With these men he hurried to Ophrah, captured all his brothers but one, and formally sacrificed them on one stone, thus securing that their blood should not, like that of Abel, cry out against him from the ground. He would have no brother near the throne, and no brother's ghost to haunt him. This done, he returned to Shechem, and was duly proclaimed king under the holy tree which was at Shechem. By this tree was a "massebah" or sacred pillar of stone. On or by this he stood, and received the acclamations of the crowd. It was at this moment that the warning voice was heard. From a safe place on Mount Gerizim the sole survivor of the seventy sons of Gideon, Jotham uttered the famous fable in which he represented Abimelech as the worthless bramble of Mount Lebanon, which yet can so easily catch fire and consume the stately cedars. The prophecy spoken, the prophet escaped to a place beyond his brother's reach.

And almost at once happens what scarcely ever fails to happen when a tyranny has been carried through. The partners in crime fall out. Buckingham conspires against Richard, and pays the penalty. As we shall see, the first victims of Dionysius of Syracuse are the men who helped him to the throne. Sometimes, it is true, they do not actually conspire; they are merely suspected of conspiracy. Or they are not even suspected; they are simply regarded as too powerful, and are therefore cut down like over-tall poppies. But whatever the cause or the pretext, it is the almost invariable rule that the first supporters of a usurper do not survive the first few months of his successful usurpation. We have seen samples in our own time.

In the case before us, the conspiracy seems to have been real. Finding, as we may imagine, the little finger of Abimelech thicker than the loins of Gideon, " the men of Shechem," taking advantage of his absence from the city, " plotted against him " ; and, it would appear, the inhabitants of the neighbouring confederate town of Thebez joined in the insurrection.

It is here that the narrative becomes especially obscure. Not only are there several names, both of men and of places, which we cannot identify, but we are given no clear indication as to the motives of the actors. We have to rely on accidental hints, and to make guesses which can at best be only probable. But it seems likely, from a single expression in the text, that Abimelech, having gained the kingship by favouring the Canaanite party, soon showed that he meant to rule the city as an Israelite—one of the intruding nation which only recently had entered the land, and which, as we know, had ere this tried to capture Shechem by an act of treachery which " Israel " himself called accursed. Having been welcomed by the Shechemites as one of themselves, he now showed favour to the Israelites, and even to the Israelites in Shechem itself, who were not full citizens, but *gērim*, strangers within the gates, corresponding roughly to the " metics " (or free non-citizens) at Athens in the fifth century. If Abimelech tried to ally himself with these to the detriment of the Canaanite aristocracy, we can easily picture the disgust of his former friends: it would be like that felt by the Roman oligarchs when Julius Cæsar gave the citizenship to the Gauls. Whatever the cause, they felt themselves betrayed; one of their own household had become their foe.

I spoke above of "the narrative". As a matter of fact there are two narratives, which the acumen of scholars has neatly separated, but which no acumen is likely ever to be able to reconcile. According to one of them, the conspirators were strengthened by the appearance of an outsider named Gaal, seemingly a Canaanite, who, despite the presence in the city of Abimelech's officer Zebul, took the lead in the revolt. "Were not," he says, "Abimelech and Zebul formerly subject to Shechem and Hamar the father of Shechem? Why then should we now be subject to him?" At the vintage-feast, the Shechemites ate and drank and reviled Abimelech, and Gaal took advantage of the feeling. "Would that I were the leader of this people: I would soon rid them of the tyrant. I would say to him, 'Make large thy army, and come forth'."

But the movement was badly managed. Foolishly leaving the city along with his supporters, Gaal is totally defeated by the skilful strategy of his enemy. He is forced back to the gate of the city, where Zebul is now ready for him, and drives him away. Of Gaal we hear no more; but a contemptuous nickname, Ben Ebed, "son of a slave", seems to show that neither Shechemite nor Israelite thenceforward thought highly of his capacity.

It would appear, if we may once more indulge in conjecture, that on this occasion Abimelech spared the offending city. He may have laid the blame of the revolt rather on Gaal than on the citizens; and it is possible that in actual fact many of the Shechemite rebels had either been killed in the battle or had been driven out with the son of the slave. In any case there were enough inhabitants left to provide a later holocaust. For, some time afterwards, a second rebellion took place: and this time there was to be no mercy. Once more the people were foolish enough—or perhaps, as so often happened in Greek history, were compelled by fear for their crops —to go out into the field; and once more Abimelech's generalship prevailed. The army was totally defeated, and after one day's hard fighting, Abimelech took the city, slaughtered the inhabitants, and—to use the expressive phrase of the historian—sowed the site with salt. Some of his enemies had escaped into a tower, which seems to have been outside the walls. Seeing that this tower was not strong enough, they removed to the temple of El-Berith—the Covenant-Baal, who watched over the place as Athene Polias protected Athens. But Baal was unequal to his task. Abimelech, bidding " every soldier hew him down a bough," piled the wood against the gate, and set the place on fire. About a thousand men and women perished in the flames.

The tyrant might thus seem to have done what one of Sulla's lieutenants told him he was in danger of doing, and left himself no subjects to rule over. But there still remained the inhabitants of Thebez. For all we know, these men, after the terrible example of Shechem, might have been willing to submit; but to Abimelech and his like revenge is insanely sweet. He attacked the city and took it, the defenders removing to a tower within the city. Once again Abimelech had recourse to fire, and came up to the gate to burn it. A woman on the roof hurled down a tile, and " all to-brake his skull "—a warning to future warriors which was remembered at least till the time of David and Uriah the Hittite. Rather than that it should be said, " A woman slew him," he bade his armourbearer run him through. Thus after three years, the reign of Abimelech ended. A grey-haired tyrant, in Palestine as in Greece, was a sight seldom seen.

The comment of the historian, if we make allowance for the Oriental style of speech, is not unlike that of Plato on Greek tyrannies, or that of Cicero on the death of Alexander of Pheræ : " Thus God requited the crime of Abimelech, which he committed against his father in slaying his seventy brethren—he made it come back on his own head—and all the wickedness of the men of Shechem God requited upon their heads ; and the curse of Jotham the son of Jerubbaal came true to them."

In the eighth chapter of the First Book of Samuel there is a speech ascribed to the great seer, picturing in very unflattering terms the character of the Israelite kingship. The speech has very slight applicability to Saul, and it is very generally supposed to be a composition of a much later time, reflecting the feelings of some Hebrew Hampden, who had suffered under the oppressions of a degenerate monarchy, such as that of Ahab or Manasseh. Be that as it may, the denunciation may glance not merely at a contemporary tyrant, but **backwards to the unforgotten wickedness of Abimelech.**

One might almost fancy that Otanes had read it, and had derived from it his conception of the evils of an uncontrolled sole rule.

"This will be the manner of the king that shall reign over you," says Samuel to the people who, crushed by the Philistines, desire a king to go out before them and fight their battles: "he will take your sons, and appoint them for his chariots and to be his horsemen, and they shall run before his chariots: and he will appoint them unto him for captains of thousands and captains of fifties: and he will set some to plough his ground, and to reap his harvest, and to make his instruments of war, and the instruments of his chariots. And he will take your daughters to be confectionaries, and to be cooks, and to be bakers. And he will take your fields, and your vineyards, and your oliveyards, even the best of them, and give them to his servants. And he will take the tenth of your seed, and of your vineyards, and give to his eunuchs and to his servants. And he will take your menservants, and your maidservants, and your goodliest herds, and your asses, and put them to his work. He will take the tenth of your flocks, and ye shall be his servants. And ye shall cry out in that day because of your king which ye shall have chosen you; and Jehovah will not answer you in that day."

In modern language, the tyrant would constrain everybody into the service of the State, and introduce conscription.

THE GREEK TYRANNIES

"The tyrant needs must court the common herd."—*Euripides*.

As I have already hinted, I do not propose to describe in detail, even in such detail as our sources of information permit, all the Greek tyrannies of which we have any account. The Greek independent cities were so numerous, and so many of these fell at some time or other under the dominion of tyrants, that the briefest description of the despotisms would take more space than I could afford for my whole subject. Paradoxically enough, I might be compelled to prolixity by the very scantiness of information. Most of the tyrannies were extinct before the times of our two great historians, whose notices of them are in the main incidental and allusive; and to form a clear idea of them from these slight references, even when eked out by the brief remarks of Aristotle, might necessitate dissertations and conjectures, which—as the reader of Grote knows—often fill more pages than plain narrative. A few typical specimens, then, are all I can choose; but these will be sufficient to enable the reader to gain a sort of composite photograph of the Tyrant, and to see how his features are reproduced, more or less exactly, whenever he reappears in history.

I have already mentioned Pheidon of Argos, the earliest Greek tyrant of whom we hear. He is, in one respect, almost unique. He was a legitimate king, bearing that unfailing mark of legitimacy, a divine lineage. As the early kings of Scandinavia or Wessex traced their line to Odin or Frey, so Pheidon's family-tree went back through fifteen generations to Heracles. Unluckily, we know neither the date of Heracles nor that of Pheidon; the chronologers differ by about a century. Roughly, we may place him seven or eight hundred years before Christ. He would, in any case, have the prestige of a long and uninterrupted succession.

But a kingship of this kind, as we learn from Homer and from the analogous Germanic sagas, involved limitation. Every Homeric king was confessed to come ultimately from the gods; but he could not do as he pleased. He had to consult his council, and, if he showed signs of arbitrariness, he ran great risk of raising a rebellion, which, in the case of Agamemnon, broke out into open mutiny. Pheidon chafed under these restrictions, loose as they were, and stretched his prerogatives so far that our authorities have no hesitation in calling him by the opprobrious name. He was, in fact, not a Cromwell, but a more energetic, and, for a time, more successful Richard II. He was a conqueror: we hear that he even made himself master of Corinth. Men had not then learnt, nor have they yet learnt, that foreign conquest is, so far as its effect on individual happiness is concerned, a mere phantom; "glory" has constantly been found by despots a very useful "ersatz" for freedom; and we may plausibly conjecture that these victories greatly strengthened Pheidon's hands.

But there is more to learn about him. He was the first Greek, we are told, to establish a convenient metal currency. He issued a copper and silver coinage. The advantage of this to a despot cannot easily be exaggerated; indeed, as I have said, there are some scholars who ascribe the existence of the early tyrannic dynasties in the main to the prevalence of this system. A mercenary soldier can be easily enlisted if a potentate is in a position to give him a wage in a form which is comparatively light to carry and which everybody understands. A shilling in the hand is worth more to a soldier than the promise of an ox, or even than the prospect of three acres and a cow when his term of service is over. Abimelech could hire a ruffian for a shekel; and Pheidon, with the command of a mint, could hire men for three years or the duration. Such men were professional soldiers; and the rest of Greece—even Sparta under the system of Lycurgus—had nothing but a militia. No wonder that for a long time Pheidon was successful in his aggressions. For some years he was certainly the chief man in the Peloponnese; and he harboured, not unreasonably, the design of ruling over all the cities which Heracles was said to have conquered. His power fell when he strained it too far. He contrived to fall out with Elis and Sparta at once; and even his mercenaries were not equal to the combination. But his example was not forgotten. His coinage was imitated by the Eubœans, and his other devices by a succession of tyrants in a score of cities.

Our next tyranny is noteworthy specially for two things, which may be regarded as the ancient equivalents of the control of the press and the establishment of a nationalist religion. These are methods familiar to despots in all ages: all know how Napoleon kept a tight hand on the newspapers, and, though restoring to the Church much of the power of which it had been deprived by the Revolution, made it, as far as possible, a department of state.

Sicyon, a very strong fortress on the Corinthian Gulf, was one of the oldest cities in Greece, and is mentioned in the Homeric " Catalogue " as at one time ruled by the hero Adrastus. Adrastus had been expelled from Argos, and took refuge in Sicyon, where, after the death of Polybus, he became king, and whence, as one of the famous " Seven against Thebes ", he set out to attack that city, on an expedition which he alone, of all the Seven, survived. After his death he became the tutelary hero of Sicyon, a kind of patron-saint, whose tomb was specially sacred.

About 676, Orthagoras, who is said to have been originally a cook, and who therefore may be guessed to have posed as a champion of the poor against the rich, overthrew the ruling oligarchy at Sicyon, and established a dynasty which lasted far longer than any other in Greek history—no less than a hundred years. About 600 his descendant, Cleisthenes, became ruler.

As the legend of Adrastus shows, there had been a close connection between Argos and Sicyon; indeed, the Dorian upper classes at Sicyon were believed to have come from Argos, and their chiefs claimed the same descent from Heracles which we have seen was the pride of the Argive ruling houses. The three most important " tribes " at Sicyon were Argive and Dorian : Cleisthenes sprang from another tribe. Having quarrelled with Argos, he determined to humiliate these tribes, and not only asserted their inferiority to his own, but gave them the mocking names of the Boars, the Asses and the Piglings. This was more than a mere insult; it was to offend these Dorians in their keenest religious sensibilities. A faint idea of its character may be gained by remembering the feelings of the Catholics in England when the Mass was profaned, and its mysteries were called a hocus-pocus.

But this was not all. As "Homer", who was then supposed to have been the author not only of the Iliad but of the Thebaid, in which the story of the Seven was told, had celebrated Adrastus, Cleisthenes determined to get rid of him: and here we may compare the proceedings of Henry VIII against the shrine of St. Thomas of Canterbury. Like St. Thomas, Adrastus was still alive, and a very present demi-god in the city. That he was also present in Argos will offer no difficulty to those who remember that "our Lady" is present simultaneously at Lourdes, at La Salette, and at Embrun: but his presence at Sicyon Cleisthenes would not tolerate so long as he protected the hated Argos. He began by applying to the oracle of Delphi, but Apollo was not favourable to the plan; Adrastus, he replied, was king of Sicyon, and Cleisthenes was a rascal. It was necessary to try other methods. The legendary enemy of Adrastus was the Theban hero Melanippus, the chief agent in repelling the Seven, and the slayer of Adrastus' son. Could Melanippus be brought to Sicyon, Adrastus, unable to bear his neighbourhood, would leave of his own accord. The Thebans consented to the transfer; Melanippus came to Sicyon, and was given a sacred enclosure in the very "Prytanēum" or Senate-house, in the strongest part of the city. Adrastus, it was assumed, took his departure; and Cleisthenes withdrew from him the tragic choruses and the solemn sacrifices. Argos and Sicyon no longer had a common religion. The effect would be, on its tiny scale, not dissimilar to that of the disestablishment and proscription of the Greek Church in Russia, or to that of the proclamation of a German Christianity in the Reich. Some centuries earlier, in a distant country, as we have observed, Jeroboam the son of Nebat "had made Israel to sin" in a like fashion; he had established, or perhaps merely patronised, the altars of Bethel and Dan in opposition to that of Jerusalem. Every tyrant knows the advantage of enlisting religion in his service, and of controlling it so that it tends to his own glory and security.

Of Cleisthenes' other achievements there is no need to speak at length. The surest means of gaining glory among the Greeks was to win at the Olympic Games, which were not merely athletic contests but services in honour of the national deity. When Alcibiades was enumerating his claims to the devotion of Athens, he put first the fact that in the chariot-race he had won the first, second, and fourth places. When, in the Peloponnesian War, the Athenians captured Dorieus of Rhodes, one of their worst enemies, they set him at liberty because he was the greatest Olympic victor of his day. Tyrants knew well how to court popularity by seeking Olympic glory for their city. A glance at a copy of Pindar's Odes will show how many followed this plan with success; and will enable us to form a conjecture as to the number who tried it and failed. Hiero of Syracuse, Theron of Agrigentum, and several leaders of ruling families, won one or other of the Olympic contests; in the Pythian Games, which were second only to the Olympic, Hiero was repeatedly victorious, and in the Nemean chariot-race his brother-in-law Chromius was successful, doubtless casting reflected glory upon the ruler. No expense was spared in the training and equipment of drivers, runners, and boxers who might thus exalt the honour of their patrons; and after the contest was over, at some solemn feast, a Pindar or a Simonides, for value received, with a choir of singers, celebrated the praises of the king in odes which have made his name immortal.

Cleisthenes, long before Hiero, pursued the same path. It suited his purposes to take part in the so-called First Sacred War,* which was undertaken to punish the city of Cirrha for its insolence to the oracle of Delphi. By his naval victory over the Cirrhæans he did much to promote the success of the allied pietists, and incidentally strengthened himself at home; for with his share of the spoils he built a magnificent portico or arcade, which he called after his own name, and which increased his prestige with the citizens. But further, he presided over the foundation of the Pythian games, which were held regularly in honour of Apollo.† At these games he himself competed,

* Similarly, two and a half centuries later, Philip of Macedon found it convenient to pose as a defender of religion, and to destroy the Phocians on the ostensible ground of their impiety. That their destruction also opened his way into Greece was a motive sufficiently obvious, though he did not avow it.

† In addition to all this, Cleisthenes made large donations to the oracle. Gifts to the gods, says Aristotle, were a recognised device of tyrants. Exactions from the people for this purpose would keep them weak and poor, while at the same time they could be represented not as taxes but as religious " benevolences." The blame, in fact, for the extortion could be cast upon the gods.

and in 582 B.C., at the second celebration, won the prize for the chariot-race.

"Bella gerant alii, tu, felix Austria, nube." The greatness of Austria was built on a number of lucky marriages, which enlarged her empire without, as a rule, great expenditure of blood. The tyrants, though they could shed blood when it seemed desirable, saw also the advantage of alliances. We shall see many instances in the sequel. Cleisthenes, having in the Sacred War seen the power of the Athenian Megacles, the head of a great family called the Alcmeonids, gave his daughter Agariste to this chief. Of this marriage Herodotus tells a romantic story. As many suitors sought the hand of this princess as wooed Penelope or Angelica; among these was the Argive Hippocleides, who had the best chance, until in a drunken frolic he danced it away. "You have lost your bride," said Cleisthenes. "Hippocleides doesn't care," replied the suitor; Agariste was given to Megacles, and the Greek language was enriched with a proverb. We shall meet Megacles again. From this marriage was born a second Cleisthenes, who, by the irony of fate, was the originator of an Athenian democratic constitution.

Of the end of the elder Cleisthenes we know nothing. But it seems to have occurred in the exact year in which Peisistratus became tyrant of Athens, 560 B.C. Whatever were the circumstances, his tyranny ceased with him. The old oligarchy was restored, and even Adrastus returned; for Herodotus tells us that in his time the hero was worshipped in the city from which he had been expelled.

Almost contemporaneous with the dynasty of Cleisthenes was a still more famous one at Corinth; one so great that, as has been said of certain famous men, history felt unable to do justice to it, and called in the aid of legend. Its founder was Cypselus, whose birth, Herodotus tells us, was foretold by an oracle. The child to be born would be the ruin of the Bacchiad clan, which was then the ruling oligarchy in the city. Accordingly like Herod, the Bacchiads determined to kill the child as soon as it should be born; but, by a divine chance, it smiled in the face of the man sent to murder it,* and he could not bring himself to do the deed. Thus it came back to its mother, who hid him in a cypsĕlĕ or corn-bin, to grow to manhood and fulfil the oracle. We can make out that he pursued the usual course; he ingratiated himself with the poorer classes, expelled by their aid the Bacchiad oligarchs, and made himself tyrant of the city, where he ruled " prosperously " for thirty years. According to the story told by the Corinthians themselves, he was harsh and cruel; " many of the citizens he drove into banishment, many he deprived of their property, and more he put to death." According to Aristotle he was popular, and needed no bodyguard. This may have been because he had left himself no enemies to fear.

His son, Periander, is still more famous, and his history is still more inextricably entangled with legend and myth. It is with him that the familiar story of Arion is connected; and it is of him that the tale is told which the Romans

* New-born babies do not smile; hence this was a proof of divine protection. It is said that Zoroaster gave the same token of his future greatness; and when Virgil, in the fourth Eclogue, says to a mysterious child who is about to be born, " Incipe, parve puer, *risu* cognoscere matrem," he seems to indicate that the child will be born more than human.

THE GREEK TYRANNIES 43

borrowed and attached to Tarquin the Proud. He sent a messenger to Thrasybulus, tyrant of Miletus, to inquire what was the best way of ruling his city. Thrasybulus said not a word, but took the envoy through a field of corn, where he cut off all the ears which overtopped the rest. Periander understood the parable, and destroyed all those leading citizens whom his father had left. Nor is this by any means the most remarkable of the stories which clustered round his name.

Amid this mass of saga we can detect some facts, and they are, as usual, characteristic of the tyrannical mind. Periander was plainly an able soldier; the dominion of Corinth was wider in his reign than ever before or since; and he even contrived to achieve a feat which might have been thought impossible. He gained, and kept, the rule over the Corinthian colonies; whereas for a mother-city to retain a hold over her colonies was practically unprecedented in the Greek world; and Corcyra, the chief of the Corinthian colonies, was in later times distinguished for the deadly hatred which it showed to its metropolis. We hear also, as we should expect, that he cultivated the favour of the gods, giving magnificent presents to Zeus of Olympia; and that he compelled his people to be industrious, so that they should have little time to plot conspiracies. As the tale of Arion shows, he was a great patron of the arts of music and poetry, and the artists repaid him in their own fashion, as Virgil and Horace repaid the favours of Augustus. Like all successful men, he had his admirers, and there were some who, confounding success with virtue, actually gave him a place among the Seven Wise

Men of Greece. Solomon is not the only monarch who has chastised his people with whips and yet has gained the repute of almost superhuman wisdom.

We now leave Corinth for Athens, and come to a man if possible more renowned than Periander.

The history of Peisistratus is particularly interesting. In the dim light that beats upon his throne, we can discern that he was a mild ruler, a patron of arts and letters, and probably not unpopular with the citizens. At the same time he has the unfailing stigmata of the tyrant; he seized the rule by force, he made it permanent, and he depended on mercenary soldiers. Thus he did not escape the censure which the Greeks invariably passed upon the tyrant, whether he exercised his tyranny well or ill. His interests were inevitably opposed to those of his people; and, disguise the truth as he might, there were men who recognised it, both in his time and afterwards.

The illustrious Solon had already given Athens a constitution; but as far as we can see, the people had not yet learned how to apply it, and the great nobles were still able to do pretty much as they pleased. Of these the three most powerful were Megacles, the head of a family on which an hereditary curse was supposed to rest, Lycurgus, and Peisistratus. Solon was alive, but aged, and the last man to wish to make himself king. In the year 560, Peisistratus, apparently exaggerating his strength, adopted a device which—with variations depending on circumstances—men desirous of establishing a tyranny have often imitated, and which Plato in his Republic notes as characteristic of such men. He appeared in his chariot, drawn by two mules, and both he and the mules were wounded. Solon saw through the trick. " You are not like Odysseus," said he, " for he wounded himself to deceive his enemies; you have wounded yourself to deceive your own countrymen." But the people were more credulous; they believed his story that he had been attacked and all but murdered by his political opponents; and in their indignation and compassion they voted him a guard of fifty clubmen. Needless to say, the clubs speedily became swords, and the fifty grew in number. He was soon able to seize the Acropolis. Megacles and his other enemies fled the city. Solon remained, a lonely patriot. " It would have been easy," he told the people, " to prevent; to cure is harder, but more glorious." But though he even donned arms, he could induce no one to follow him; and, saying that he at least had done his duty, he gave up the struggle. For safety, he said, he relied on his old age: he seems to have been close on eighty; and, on that account, Peisistratus spared his life.

But the tyrant had miscalculated his strength. Megacles and Lycurgus united their forces, and drove him into exile. Had they remained harmonious, he might never have returned; but after a time—how long we do not know—they quarrelled; and Megacles made overtures to the exile. It was then that the famous stratagem was tried—a woman dressed as the goddess Athene declaring that the city, if it desired the favour of the deity, must bring back her banished. One of the terms of the alliance was that Peisistratus should marry Megacles' daughter; and marry her he did, but, fearful of the curse on the family, he left her a wife in name only. Megacles, exasperated by this insult, made peace with Lycurgus, and once more drove the tyrant into exile; and on this occasion he was absent no less than ten years.

Tyrants have a fellow-feeling towards other tyrants.* In the island of Naxos an oligarch named Lygdamis had allied himself with the common people against the richer classes, and thus made himself ruler of both. During these years, Lygdamis gave valuable aid in men and money to Peisistratus, in the expectation, which proved well-founded, that if ever he was in a similar difficulty, Peisistratus would aid him in return. Mercenaries were hired, and the two despots landed on the memorable plain of Marathon. The battle was short; it would seem that there were traitors in the Athenian camp. At any rate, Peisistratus, almost without losing a man, scattered the opposing army, and for the third time entered the city in triumph. He was careful to propitiate the gods. The sacred city of Delos was purified; the houses of the accursed family of Megacles were destroyed, and the bones of all its buried members were exhumed and cast out of the city.

From this time onward he ruled in peace, and with

* Thus Aristodemus, tyrant of Cumæ, gave assistance and a refuge to Tarquin the Proud in his exile. The history of Aristodemus shows all the usual signs which mark the tyrant. He cultivated the favour of the people, earned a high repute in war, and used his position to gain sole rule. He then banished or massacred every man who was likely to prove dangerous. During the next few years he paid great attention to the education of youth, which was directed to enervating their character, and to making them slavish in their disposition, and thus ever more willing to submit to a single will. Fortunately, there were some left whom he had not reduced to " old feeble carrions or such suffering souls that welcome wrongs." The people at last rose, and after a desperate conflict got rid of their oppressor.

moderation. Thucydides, who, it is true, was of his family, tells us what he was content with levying a tax of five per cent. on the incomes of the people. Some say that he once even allowed himself to be put on trial before the Areopagus; but as he had now a large army of Thracian mercenaries, it would appear that the risk of condemnation was slight. He was in as little danger as Bothwell when tried for the murder of Darnley by an unarmed court when he had a threatening band of Borderers at his back. But Herodotus, who was not inclined to favour despots, agrees with Thucydides; and even Aristotle does not altogether dissent, though he tells us that Peisistratus, in undertaking great public buildings, had the object of impoverishing his subjects, whose business it was to pay for them. Perhaps, like the Hebrews under Solomon, they did not for some time perceive that the splendid edifices, which they admired so highly, were really oppressions in disguise. He certainly improved the city, as Napoleon III improved Paris, when his architect Haussman gave the citizens wide and beautiful streets, which incidentally could be easily commanded by cannon.

Many other achievements are ascribed to him. He is said to have had the poems of Homer collected, arranged, edited, and recited throughout at the great " Panathenaic " festival; a statement which has excited almost as much controversy as the question of free-will and determinism. To use the words of Chaucer.

> " In scole is gret altercacioun
> In this matere, and gret disputisoun,
> And hath ben, of an hundred thousand men."

He is said also to have formed a library, which Xerxes,

in spite of the haste with which he left Athens after Salamis, took care to carry with him to Persia. This library, the first ever formed in Greece, he threw open to the public. He encouraged the earliest tragedian, Thespis, to whom Solon had refused permission to play. So far as we can see, the works of Thespis were crude enough; but his literary son was Phrynichus, no mean poet, and the pupil of Phrynichus was the mighty Aeschylus. On the whole, then, Peisistratus was certainly a great ruler. Even if these stories are fables, fables like them are not told about small men. As Thirlwall says, he gave the people repose; and that repose may well have had much to do with the greatness they attained soon after his dynasty was swept away.

His power descended to his sons, of whom Hippias was the eldest, Hipparchus the second. Hipparchus was murdered by two friends, Harmodius and Aristogeiton, who, like many other people, have gained a glory to which they are not entitled; for the murder was due to a mere private quarrel. Not unnaturally, Hippias became more severe after it; and the following four years of his reign were a tyranny in our sense of the word. He was actually expelled by the Spartan king Cleomenes, who was urged to the act by the family of Megacles and by an oracle of Delphi. Nevertheless, the Athenians persisted in regarding Harmodius and Aristogeiton as protagonists of liberty; their statues were erected in the city, and a famous "scolion" (or drinking song) "In myrtle-boughs I wreathe my sword," commemorated for all time their imaginary deed.

As Hippias had provided himself with a place of

refuge for precisely such an emergency, one might have thought that he would be content. But he nursed his hopes of returning for no less than twenty years. He very nearly did return. The Spartans speedily repented of their action, when they discovered that the Alcmeonids had very skilfully manipulated the oracle of Delphi in their own favour, and that there were other prophecies declaring (as it happened, truly) that a free Athens would be a menace to Sparta. They therefore sent for Hippias, and proposed to their allies to restore him by force of arms. Probably they would have done so, had not Sosicles the Corinthian risen and told the assembly the story of Cypselus and Periander, and their cruelties, ending up with the words, " Such, Lacedæmonians, is tyranny, and to such deeds does tyranny lead. Greatly did we of Corinth marvel when we first heard that you had sent for Hippias ; and we marvel still more to hear your words now. By the common gods of Greece we urge you not to set up despots in her cities. And if you persist in your resolve to do so, and most unjustly to restore Hippias, know this at least, that we of Corinth shall not approve your designs." In spite of a reply from Hippias, in which he, too, appealed to the gods, and made full use of his extraordinary knowledge of oracles and their interpretation, the enterprise was renounced, and Hippias retired to Sigeum in the Troad, which Peisistratus had taken the precaution to secure.

Another chance came some years later. In the reign of Darius the Ionian Greeks revolted against Persia, and the Athenians gave them very effective aid. Darius **vowed vengeance**, and bade a slave repeat every day in his ears, " Sire, remember the Athenians." He did not forget them, and in 490 sent a great armament to punish the city. Hippias joined the expedition, and acted as its guide. He directed the Persians, or rather the mixed host of forty-six nations which composed the army, to the very plain of Marathon from which he had so easily marched with his father nearly fifty years before. Herodotus tells a romantic tale. The night before the battle, Hippias dreamt that he lay in his mother's arms —that is, as he supposed, that he would soon return to his native city. But it was not to be. Next day, he had a fit of coughing, and a tooth fell out. No search could find it. " The earth that covers the tooth," said Hippias, " is all that I shall ever regain." He was right. The battle of Marathon destroyed all his hopes, and started a democratic Athens on a career of almost unparalleled glory.

Of Polycrates, the tyrant of Samos, I need say little; for everybody has heard of him, as the very type of amazing good-fortune and of sudden and utter ruin. Who does not know how, to propitiate the Nemesis that punishes good luck, he threw his ring into the sea, and how it miraculously came back to him; how Amasis of Egypt, hearing of this, conceived that the gods must be preparing a terrible disaster for him and renounced his alliance; and how, for no known reason, he was inveigled to the mainland by a Persian satrap and put to death? He concerns us here on other accounts. He made himself ruler by the help of his two brothers, and having gained his purpose, killed one and banished the other. This was in the true tyrannic style; for a tyrant always distrusts his friends, and bears, like the Turk, no brother near the throne. Having gained the tyranny, he kept it by external conquest; indeed he is reckoned by Thucydides among the great "thalassocrats" or naval masters of the Ægean, the successor of Minos of Crete and the precursor of the tyrant city of Athens. So strong was he that he even repelled an invasion of the Samian exiles, which was aided by Sparta herself. In his own island his public works, adopted as a means of at once occupying and impoverishing the people, made Samos the most magnificent city in Greece; and he drew the gods to his side by consecrating to Apollo the island of Rheneia. He patronised poetry, and Anacreon was his laureate; though we hear that the bard was less successful in his court-poems than in those in which he celebrated wine and women.* Altogether, in spite of his terrible end, he was as representative a tyrant as it is easy to find.

With him I must close my account of the tyrannies of Greece proper, though there were many others of whom something might be said—Theagenes of Megara, Thrasybulus of Miletus, and, in later times the infamous Alexander of Pheræ, whose own wife found it desirable to get rid of him. I pass to another part of the Hellenic world, in which, though the character of the Greek colonists had been to some extent affected by contact with the native population, yet the nature of the tyrant appears remarkably identical. "Caelum, non animum, mutant qui trans mare currunt." Something might be said of the tyrants of Greek Italy, or "Magna Græcia." It will be sufficient to speak of those of Sicily.

* After the death of Polycrates, Anacreon went to Athens, and paid the same homage to Hipparchus.

SICILY

"Necesse est multos timeat quem multi timent."—*Laberius.*

FROM about the middle of the eighth century to about the end of the seventh, a stream of emigration set forth from Greece proper to Sicily and Magna Græcia. Greece, a poor and mountainous country, has always found it difficult to feed its people from its own resources, and emigrations have been frequent, though never more so than in these early times. In Asia Minor, and all round the Black Sea, were Greek colonies: these, for various reasons, were found insufficient, and the stream turned westward. No country was more attractive than the great and fertile land of Sicily, where there was only a barbarous people, at least in the eastern half, to dispute the territory, and where, so we are told, some Greeks had settled as early as the time of the Trojan War. On its small scale, the migration might be compared to the rush to America in the seventeenth century of our era, different as were the causes which provoked it.

Had there been philosophic historians in those days, there might have been discussions as to the effect which contact with uncivilised tribes, and distance from the mother country, might have upon the intruders. Some changes might have been observed; but on the whole Greeks remained Greeks. In Sicily we find, as in Greece proper, a number of separate cities, very jealous of their independence, and unable to agree even though all around them were the Sicels among whom they had thrust themselves, and who might at any time become a great danger to them. Besides this, there was, especially in the west of the island, the great power of Carthage, which, about 600 B.C., ceased to be content with the possession of a few trading-factories, and aspired to the actual conquest of the island. It is probable that Carthage would have succeeded in this design if she had firmly persisted in it; but she was far more deeply interested in trade than in conquest; and, so soon as a victory had secured her mercantile interests, her merchant-princes, dreading the enormous expenditure which mercenary armies entailed, drew back. Her policy, in fact, was somewhat like that of our early East India Company, which fought when trade was endangered and kept the peace when trade seemed safe.

Internally, conditions were, so far as we can judge, more or less what they always are when a "civilised" race has imposed itself on a "barbarous" one—that is, on one with inferior armaments or skill in war. The Sicels, in places where they were thoroughly reduced, became hewers of wood and drawers of water for their conquerors; at best they were serfs, at worst slaves. Above them were free Greek landowners, some large, some small. The cities were, in the main, like the burghs of the early English, places of refuge from attack, or centres of administration, but, as all of then were on or near the sea, they could partially maintain themselves by commerce—which was still, like that of Drake or Hawkins, not always easily distinguished from freebooting; and there was constantly growing an urban population, or "Demos", which the oligarchs refused to recognise, but which, like the "plebs" in ancient Rome, often demanded recognition and could, by adding itself either to discontented oligarchs or to the smaller land-owners, make itself very troublesome. But, in comparison with the great cities or countries of to-day, it is hardly an exaggeration to declare that in Greek Sicily there was hardly a commercial or trading middle-class at all. The government was therefore, with short interludes, oligarchical—that is, it was in the hands of a few wealthy families, which, so long as they agreed among themselves, did as they pleased, and, so long as they were not excessively oppressive, did what they pleased without serious opposition. To compare small things with great, we may liken the society to that of the Southern States of America before the Civil War. As in those States, there was a proud and dominant upper class, with the virtues and vices which usually attend pride and dominance; resting on slave-labour, and therefore despising manual toil; fond of war and pleasure, but capable of generosity and nobility so long as its privileges and property were not threatened. By the side of the aristocrats and the slaves there was also a class which in the States was hardly more highly regarded than the slaves—that of the "poor whites"; in Sicily the sort of men without any close ties of nation or family, who drift, as necessity or inclination leads it, into the cities, and especially into maritime cities. These would be at the disposal of any ambitious man who could play on their discontent and promise them an improvement in their position at the expense of their betters; ready and willing to accept his pay and to serve against any enemy. Not seldom the enemy was the ruling oligarchy of the city in which these despised people dwelt. With nothing to lose, and a chance of much to gain, they welcomed revolution even if it meant anarchy. Troubled waters were their natural fishing-ground.

While the oligarchs held together, these dangerous elements might be kept in their place. But, in the confined space of the cities, disputes were constantly arising, and the families quarrelled in the Sicilian cities as the Orsini and the Colonna quarrelled in mediæval Rome, or as next-door neighbours fought in the Rhine towns: and here was the opportunity of the man of daring and determination. It was thus that Phalaris made himself master of Agrigentum, posing as the friend of the poor against the rich, and promising a golden age to those who would follow him. When he had won his victory, savagery was a necessity, for his partisans had to be paid, and payment could be given only in the form of loot. The wealthy must be slaughtered, and their property divided. Such a necessity it was that overcame the scruples of William the Conqueror himself. To his followers the invasion was a business-speculation; when by their aid it had succeeded, they demanded their dividends. Similarly, but far more ruthlessly, Phalaris paid his helpers. But slaughter breeds slaughter. A tyrant never knows whether he has killed enemies enough; every murder means more suspicion; and, like Macbeth, the usurper thinks always that one more murder, and one more after that, will make him safe. " He is in blood stepped in so far that, should he wade no more, returning were as tedious as go o'er." Thus the Sicilian tyrants became a proverb for cruelty; and the name of Phalaris is infamous among an infamous crew. He had to rule by terror; and the story of the Brazen Bull remains to make him the very type and symbol of the terrorist. But the time came when the terrorism made the timid brave; and a sudden conspiracy ended Phalaris and his despotism together.

When once the tyranny had been gained, foreign war was necessary in order to keep the mercenaries employed, and to delude the citizens with glory. "A great reputation," said Napoleon, "is nothing but a big noise"; a victory at pretty regular intervals prevents people from feeling their chains; and an indemnity or a sack helps to bolster up shaky finances. We know that Phalaris was a good soldier, and it may have been this that kept him so long on his throne. For another Sicilian dynasty military skill did still more, and enabled it, in some measure, to dispense with terrorism. This was the Gelonian dynasty, which, though it lasted less than twenty years, has gained a fame inferior to none.

Gelo, unlike many other tyrants, was of good birth. He distinguished himself as a general in the service of Hippocrates, tyrant of Gela. When Hippocrates died, the Geloans refused to acknowledge his sons as rulers, and broke out into rebellion. Gelo, shocked at their disloyalty, put down the mutiny by main force; and then, when the need of pretence was gone, threw off the mask, deposed the princes, and reigned in their stead.

He was thus master of Gela; but a combination of circumstances enabled him to extend his power to other cities. The Greek factions were never unwilling to seek help from the corresponding factions elsewhere. Their patriotism, though probably far more intense than ours to-day, was really not so much love of their country as devotion to a party. Thus the democrats of Megara or Samos would apply to the democracy of Athens in order to ruin the Megarian or Samian oligarchs, while the " Few " in Platæa invited the Thebans into their city, in time of peace, in order to crush the " Many "; and an exile from a city might ere long be found in the army of the city's deadly enemy. It happened that, in Syracuse, the oligarchical families were in great danger of being overthrown by the serf-cultivators, who had allied themselves with the small proprietors and, apparently, with the poor within the city: and the endangered wealthy called Gelo to their assistance. He was only too willing to consent. He came with a strong army; the Syracusan democrats, hopeless of success, yielded without striking a blow; and then Gelo, instead of restoring the oligarchs to power, quietly threw them over, and made himself tyrant over rich and poor alike. Doubtless, like that other despot of whom we hear, who, having promised a poet a large sum for an ode and then refused it, Gelo considered he had done enough for his friends by giving them the pleasures of hope. He next enlarged the city by a series of transportations which remind us of those so often carried out by Assyrian conquerors. Thousands of people were brought in from Gela, and from the Sicilian Megara some hundreds; but when the

Megarian "Demos" arrived, he sold the whole number as slaves, allowing "freedom" only to their betters. He had, says Herodotus, the fixed belief that Demos was an uncomfortable bedfellow; whereas wealthy people do not as a rule rebel as long as they think their property is safe.

By these means Syracuse became the biggest city in Sicily; and it was a city of freemen and serfs only; the "plebs", which had before been increasing in numbers, was reduced to impotence. Hence a phenomenon which we shall notice repeatedly, that though, at fairly regular intervals, a democratic constitution was set up in Syracuse, it was always weak, and never lasted long. What was perhaps worse, it was always timid and suspicious. When war threatened from without, it was afraid to trust the oligarchs with military power, and thus brought the whole city to the brink of ruin, from which it was saved only by an extraordinary series of accidents. Of this ever-present fear an ambitious and able man was constantly ready to take advantage, and the Demos thus exchanged the King Log they dreaded for a King Stork whom they found considerably worse.

In the time of Gelo, European Greece was in terrible danger from the threatened invasion of Xerxes, and the nation, for a short while, remembered that in spite of all its dissensions, it was yet, in a fashion, *one*. Multitudes of men were willing to try their chances in a safer part of the Greek world; they migrated to Italy or to Sicily, and were only too ready to take service with anyone who would employ them. Gelo was thus able to increase his mercenary army, and even to form a great navy.

His power was immense. His brother Hiero ruled in Gela, and trusty friends in other cities; while tribute came in from many places, and the estates of dispossessed landowners provided him with large sums. So high was his reputation that, as the threat of Persian invasion drew nearer, the European Greeks asked for aid from him as the most likely man to be able to give aid that was worth having: and he, confident in his position, refused to give it unless he was appointed commander-in-chief of the whole Hellenic force.

Exactly at the same time, he had his own dangers to face; for a great Carthaginian army under Hamilcar landed at Palermo and besieged the city of Himera. It is said by some that this invasion was made in concert with the Persians, in order to prevent Sicily from providing just that assistance which Gelo had been asked to afford. At any rate it banished any idea of the kind. It is significant, and characteristic of the tyrannic spirit, that the Carthaginians were called in by Terillus, the tyrant of Himera, himself. If he hoped by their means to increase his power, he was disappointed; for Gelo, advancing to the rescue of the city, was able, by that mixture of skill and good fortune to which victories are usually due, to defeat the Carthaginians with enormous slaughter. According to a calculation which was naturally very gladly accepted, this battle was said to have been fought on the same day as Salamis, and it gained for Gelo as much glory as Salamis did for Themistocles. But, while Salamis started democratic Athens on a course of splendour scarcely equalled in history, the day of Himera, which was a tyrannic victory, had no comparable effect. Soon afterwards, Gelo died, and his brother Hiero succeeded him at Syracuse.

Hiero will always be remembered, for he was celebrated by one of the greatest of all lyric poets. His Olympic and Pythian victories were sung by Pindar, who did not forget to allude flatteringly to the great naval victory off Cumae, which broke the sea-power of the Etruscans, and thus prepared the way for the advance of Rome: a victory commemorated in an inscription which still exists. Hiero's dominion was not less wide, or less imposing, than Gelo's; but it illustrates a rule which has scarcely an exception. Even if the founder of a tyrannical dynasty should contrive to be tolerably mild, his successors are not so; and all the evidence goes to prove that Hiero was harsh and oppressive. We cannot believe that the inhabitants of Catana, whom he expelled in order to make room for the citizens of his new city of Aetna, which he built to gain the glory of an Oecist or Founder, regarded him as particularly merciful. He showed also that common tyrannic mark, a hatred of his brother Polyzelus, of whose popularity he was jealous, and whom he sought to kill. It is said that the poet Simonides reconciled the fraternal foes. " It is hard," says Simonides in one of his poems, " to quit oneself like a truly good man." He must have found it still harder to induce a despot to quit himself in that fashion. The chief claim of Hiero to respect is that he more than once interfered to prevent or punish the atrocities of other tyrants—generally with the intention of aggrandising himself at their expense.

After his death the usual degeneracy rapidly showed

itself. His brother Thrasybulus, and his nephew, the son of Gelo, disputed the rule. Thrasybulus adopted the simple plan of allowing, or encouraging, the youth to ruin himself by luxury, waste, and all sorts of corrupting pleasures, and then gradually pushed him out of the way. He was now able to behave like himself; that is, to banish or murder wealthy citizens and seize their property, and to make himself universally detested. A general revolt was the result; he was driven from the outer city of Achradina, and forced to take refuge in the inner fortress of Ortygia. Here he might have hoped to maintain himself permanently; but the insurgents, gaining help from the whole island, were able to blockade him and finally to compel him to capitulate. He was allowed to resign and depart; and his mercenaries, whom it would appear he was no longer able to pay, departed with him, and scattered over the island. He himself retired to Locri in the south of Italy; but the Gelonian dynasty was declared deposed and proclaimed the common foe of Sicilian freedom, for ever incapable of reigning. This was only eighteen years after it was established by Gelo. In so short a time can a rule, once welcomed as the salvation of a country, debase itself and perish to the delight of all.

After some further troubles, a democratic government was set up not only in Syracuse but in every Greek city of Sicily. It would appear, however, that the times were not ripe for it. So far as we can judge from the meagre accounts that have come down to us, oligarchies again came into power, and—though democracies here and there reappeared—were able either to retain their position or to recover it when dispossessed. Thus at the time of the Athenian invasion, fifty years after Thrasybulus, we find a democracy in Syracuse; but very shortly afterwards it has vanished, and an oligarchy has taken its place. Doubtless this had not happened without arousing much ill-feeling in the popular party; and it was possible, as I now go on to tell, for an energetic and unscrupulous man to avail himself of this feeling, to crush the oligarchy, and to make himself, by the familiar devices, ruler of both the Few and the Many. This man was Dionysius, the son of Hermocrates, of all Greek tyrants unquestionably the most remarkable, and the one who starts to the mind of ancient writers whenever they contemplate the phenomenon of tyranny. He began from a very low position, and in a few years, by craft and determination, raised himself to an almost unparalleled height of glory. No Greek till the time of Philip of Macedon (if indeed Philip can be called a Greek) ruled over so wide a territory; and he ruled over it for nearly forty years, dying in his bed, and leaving his kingdom to his son. He has also that significant mark of greatness: anecdotes, true or false, cling to his name. His life was written by an intimate friend, who, one might imagine, would be free from superstitious reverence: but even he could not help recording miraculous stories of his hero's early days. He wrote, and plainly believed, that such a career must have been foreboded in the eternal counsels of the gods. "The mother of Dionysius," says Philistus—and Philistus, according to Cicero, was a sound and trustworthy historian—"just before his birth, dreamt that she brought forth a Satyr. She inquired the meaning of the portent, and the Galeotæ (the official interpreters of omens) replied that the child about to be born would be the most renowned of Greeks, and that his good fortune would be lasting." Nor was this the only omen of his coming greatness. Shortly before he began to reign, he happened to be passing through the territory of Leontini, not far from Syracuse, when his horse fell into a river, and he was unable, despite his utmost exertions, to get it out. He went on his way, says Philistus, sad at heart. But he had not gone far, when he heard a neighing behind him, and turning round saw the horse once more. On its mane a swarm of bees had settled; and a swarm of bees, as everyone knows, is a portent of good luck.

His fame has lasted down to our own times; for who has not heard the story of Damon and Phintias, whose affection for each other was so great that Dionysius pardoned them both? and equally familiar is the tale of the sword of Damocles, a proverb of the uncertainty of the lives of those who have lifted themselves above their fellows. As Laberius said of Cæsar, " Necesse est multos timeat, quem multi timent." With all his power, Dionysius was in constant terror. Rather than trust himself to a barber, he used to singe his own hair with a burning coal.

He is indeed the typical tyrant, and is repeatedly referred to by Aristotle as such, especially as the type of those who rose to tyranny by the arts of the demagogue and the orator. Having gained power, he maintained it in the usual ways. He adorned Syracuse with magnificent temples and other public buildings, so that for a time it surpassed Athens itself. He sent embassies to Olympia and Delphi, and contributed largely to their funds. He patronised poets, and though, unlike his predecessor Hiero, he had no Pindar to praise him, he found many to celebrate him with less immortal eulogies. He wrote poetry himself, and even gained the prize for tragedy at Athens. Above all, he cultivated the society of philosophers, not merely of sycophants like Damocles, but of independent thinkers like the Pythagoreans. Even Plato visited him, perhaps fancying that he had found in him the " philosopher-king " of his Utopian dreams; but the visit was not altogether a success. Plato spoke out too plainly; the despot, losing his temper, is even said to have sold his Mentor as a slave. This may be a mere legend; but it is certain that Plato had to leave the city somewhat precipitately, and more than probable that the tyrant wrote a tragedy against him. The intercourse between philosophy and absolutism is generally uneasy. We think of Voltaire and Frederick the Great.

Such being the character of this extraordinary man, it cannot be undesirable to consider his career in some detail. As with every other person who has made himself a ruler, circumstances favoured him. No Napoleon could have arisen in the days of Louis XIV., and even a Marlborough never contemplated the deposition of Queen Anne. But it is only energy and determination that can turn even favourable circumstances to one's own advantage.

The leading Syracusan statesman at the time of the Athenian invasion of Sicily was Hermocrates, the son of Hermon; and it was his wise counsels that contributed mainly to the awful disaster in which the invasion ended.

Afterwards, he was sent with a squadron of ships to assist the Spartans in completing the ruin of Athens, which was expected to follow speedily. But things turned out otherwise. Athens defended herself with astonishing courage. In 410, three years after the Athenian débâcle, the Spartan fleet, with the Syracusan contingent, was totally defeated and destroyed. Hermocrates was, so far as we can see, in no way to blame for the disaster; but the opposing party at home took advantage of it to carry a sentence of banishment against him. To this he was by no means inclined to submit; he returned to Sicily, gathered an army, and attacked Syracuse, hoping for help from his partisans within the city. Among those who fought on his side was a young clerk or civil servant named Dionysius—perhaps a relative of Hermocrates. The enterprise utterly failed; Hermocrates was killed, and his supporters were banished. Dionysius would have been banished with them, but he had been so severely wounded that he was supposed to be dead.

About the same time Sicily as a whole was in the utmost danger. A Carthaginian army, under a great general named Hannibal, had stormed and sacked two important cities and was now besieging Agrigentum, a town hardly second to Syracuse itself. During the siege Hannibal died, but his successor Himilco carried on the work, and in the year 406 Agrigentum, despite the help given by Syracuse, was captured, and given over to plunder. The peril was drawing very near.

Here was the opportunity of Dionysius. He stood forward in the assembly, and ferociously attacked the government and the generals who had failed to save the second city in the island. They were not merely incompetent but traitorous; it was not the Carthaginian arms, but Carthaginian money, which had overcome them; and they would betray Syracuse in the same way. "Do not even try them," he cried amid the shouts of his partisans; "seize them and kill them here and now!" Some say the unhappy men were stoned to death at once; in any case they lost their offices, and Dionysius was chosen general with a number of colleagues. The sham-demagogue had thus taken his first step.

The second, as is usual in such cases, was to get rid of his colleagues. They too, it appeared, were traitors, accepting Punic gold, and selling their country for gain. That the charge was preposterous did not matter; the people, mad with fear, were willing to believe anything; and Dionysius vigorously fed their fears. "Nous sommes trahis," he cried constantly; and men listened to him as the Jacobins listened to Robespierre when he charged Danton with being the suborned agent of Pitt. "To save the city," he went on, "restore the Hermocrateans; they alone are honest, and they alone can stand up against Carthage." And the exiles returned; and Dionysius had now with him a body of devoted friends. With their aid a decree was passed making him sole general; it was plainly better that one man should rule than many; and the new Abimelech became not merely commander-in-chief but single commander, with absolute control of the army. Next came a vote doubling the pay of the soldiers, and thus making mutiny unlikely.

But this was only the beginning. Syracuse was still

democratic; and, though the Hermocrateans ensured him a strong body of supporters, it was far from impossible that the assembly, waking from its dream, might rescind the vote it had given in panic. Very soon, in fact, his jealous ear seemed to catch the whisperings of repentance. He was as yet only a dictator, an officer appointed for a time, and he might at any moment be called upon to lay down his power. To turn the dictatorship into a tyranny, the essence of which was permanence, he needed something further. With this end he formed an ingenious plan.

Not far away was the city of Leontini, once independent, but now a mere suburb of Syracuse. It was at present in no danger from Carthage, whose army had a totally different objective. Nevertheless, Dionysius collected a large force, and marched in that direction. When a short distance from the city, he engineered an imaginary conspiracy against his life, and " escaped " with a number of trusty adherents to the citadel. Next day he convened a meeting, and with the full power of his demagogic eloquence decribed the dangers from which he had so narrowly saved himself. His enemies, he declared, had kindled fires, and all but burned him alive in his tent. It was necessary that the saviour of his country should be, for the future, delivered from such perils. A decree was therefore passed, allowing him a guard of six hundred men. This body he at once equipped with the most modern weapons, and promised to it the most liberal pay. It is needless to add that when he had this force at his command, he found it easy to enlarge it. The " little one " speedily became a thousand; and ere long he was able to enlist a permanent standing army, with officers and men all devoted to himself.

Thus set safely above the law, he marched back to Syracuse, and pitched his camp in Ortygia, the strongest quarter of the city, which commanded the harbour, and was admirably placed for holding down the other districts. He was now tyrant in the full sense of the word; though he still thought it desirable that the Assembly should vote the death of the two most powerful of his remaining enemies. These two men were rich. It is usually men of wealth that a despot finds it convenient to put out of the way, especially when he has an expensive army to maintain.

The murders accomplished, he married the daughter of Hermocrates, and gave his sister to Hermocrates' brother Polyxenus.

We need not follow the rest of the history—a complicated and chequered tale. It was of course necessary for Dionysius to justify his existence by saving his country from Carthage. In this at first he totally failed. Himilco captured Gela and Camarina, and Dionysius, in his turn, was accused of treachery. Ere long, Syracuse itself was beseiged, and much of it was actually captured. At this moment, however, the gods intervened, as they so often did intervene in ancient sieges. We know how the "Angel of the Lord" went forth in the camp of Sennacherib by Pelusium, and smote a hundred and four score and five thousand. A similar angel went forth from the marshes outside Syracuse, and destroyed an almost equal number of Himilco's army. Dionysius was rescued by the plague, and made an agreement with

Himilco that he should remove the remnant of his host without hindrance. The blow weakened Carthage for a generation; and Dionysius had time to consolidate his power.

He knew well how to busy the minds of men with foreign quarrels, and how to delude them with the phantom of military glory. As Napoleon III, within two years of assuming the imperial crown, found it advisable to make war on Russia, so Dionysius made war on the Italian Greeks, and, when Carthage appeared feeble enough, renewed the struggle with her. With Sparta, now, after the defeat of Athens, a tyrant-city, he made an alliance. He thus had the rare fortune of retaining his power till his death, and of leaving it to his son. How the younger Dionysius lost it, and—as it is said—had to retire to Corinth and make a living by opening a school, is a tale too well-known to need repetition here.

There is another Syracusan tyrant, an account of whom may well form a transition to a study of the Italian despots of the Renaissance; for his career attracted the interest, and almost shocked the feelings, of no less a man than Machiavelli, hardened as he was to the contemplation of ambitious villainy: and he drew a comparison between the ancient prince and one whom he may possibly have personally known. He recognised the kinship between the two men, and marked how difference of time and place left them still the same in all essentials. From considering them, and others like them, he made a set of rules for the successful conduct of the tyrant's business, rules which have been the Decalogue of despotism since his time, but which, like other maxims, were merely the reduction to theory of what had been again and again exemplified in practice.

"Speaking," says Machiavelli, "of the criminal and atrocious fashion in which a principate may be attained, I will illustrate it by two examples, one ancient, the other modern. And my ancient example shall be Agathocles the Sicilian, who, starting from a lowly and even abject position, became king of Syracuse; a man without faith, without pity, without religion; the betrayer of his friends, the murderer of his fellow-citizens; yet great of soul, able to bear and overcome adversity, and thus not inferior to the greatest captains in history."

The career of Agathocles, whatever one may think of his character, is certainly wonderful. He shows all the tyrannic characteristics raised to a higher power: cruelty and ruthlessness in extreme measure, a disregard for the misery of others which appals the most cynical, energy and daring almost superhuman.

The illustrious Timoleon had put down the tyranny of the younger Dionysius, and sent, as I have just said, the tyrant to teach a school in Corinth. He had then established in Syracuse a moderate form of popular government; but once again, it would seem, democracy had failed to suit the time or the place. An oligarchy, we do not know by what means, had once more gained power, and used it with harshness and violence. This government, learning that Crotona, in South Italy, was in danger from its Bruttian neighbours, sent an expedition to its help. Among the generals was Antander, the son of Carcinus, and a subordinate officer was Antander's brother Agathocles. Carcinus was a potter—and to Machiavelli a potter might well seem "lowly"; but the position, so early gained by his two sons would indicate that he was not "abject". In any case Agathocles soon earned distinction; his personal bravery and military talents could not be hid, and apparently aroused jealousy in the government, which, like all oligarchies, distrusted exceptional ability. He expected the prize for valour; but it was refused him and given to another—probably because the other would be less dangerous. Enraged at this slight, he took the course so often taken by ambitious men, and accused his enemies of ambition and corruption. In the Assembly he furiously attacked the rulers, charging them in nobly indignant terms, with aiming at a despotism. After that, as he did not meet with sufficient support, he found it desirable to leave the city; and maintained himself as a condottiere during several years, serving, as occasion arose, with this city or that in the wars which then as ever afflicted the unhappy island. Two attempts which he made to force a return to Syracuse utterly failed; but, by a sudden revolution within the city, the oligarchs were overthrown, and he was recalled. It would appear that the revolutionaries had, after a not uncommon practice in the tangles of Sicilian diplomacy, enlisted the support of Carthage in their enterprise; it is at any rate certain that Agathocles, who stuck at nothing, was at the moment in alliance with Hamilcar the Carthaginian general. Hamilcar, hoping that if he could restore the exile in his home, he would have him as friend, and thus remove so powerful a city as Syracuse from the list of the enemies of Carthage, used all his influence to bring about the restoration, and actually presided at the ceremony which followed. Nothing, in appearance, could have been more satisfactory for the two parties, who little knew how soon both of them would regret it. At a public meeting, held in the temple of the national goddess, Agathocles swore the oath which, to Sicilians, was like the oath by the river Styx which bound Zeus himself. He would be a faithful citizen and servant of the State, with heart, soul, and strength he would defend and uphold the new constitution, and—not least important in that troubled and dangerous time—he would maintain peace with Carthage. The people believed him as he stood with uplifted hand by the sacred fire—they could not imagine that such an oath could be broken. They elected him general; whereupon he suddenly turned upon the senators, charged them with plotting his death, and slew them all. Nor was this enough; he gave *carte blanche* to his soldiers to kill any of the citizens they pleased; and four thousand of them were massacred without mercy.

Having thus got rid of his enemies, and of a number of others whom the soldiers had killed for private reasons or none, Agathocles added a farce to the tragedy. He summoned a meeting, threw aside his military cloak, and proclaimed his anxious wish to retire into private life. The citizens, however, had still sufficient independence to refuse him a request which he obviously did not intend to be taken seriously. They unanimously gave their general absolute powers and removed from him the encumbrance of colleagues.

Having broken his oath to his countrymen, it was not

to be expected that he should keep peace with the foreigner. Ere long, he was at war with Carthage ; and it is now that he shows to the full his determination and resourcefulness. It has been said that the true greatness of a general is revealed most clearly by his behaviour in disaster. If this is true, no general was ever greater than Agothocles. In his encounter with the Carthaginians he suffered a crushing defeat, which by itself would have broken the spirit of most of those whom history has called indomitable. Worse followed ; Syracuse was besieged by land and sea, and it seemed impossible for her to save herself. In this crisis Agathocles conceived a design of almost unparalleled daring. That it involved another massacre did not trouble him. Sixteen hundred of the richer citizens were slain, and their property was seized to provide funds : the temples were robbed, women were stripped of their ornaments, and " benevolences " were exacted from merchants whom it did not seem desirable to kill. Slaves were enrolled among his soldiers. From such families as survived, he chose the heirs as hostages. By these means, he equipped a fleet of sixty ships, and crowded it with soldiers. With this armament he slipped out of the harbour, outpaced the Carthaginian pursuers, and landed in Africa. Here to convince the soldiers that they must conquer or die, he solemnly burnt the ships—an act which has become proverbial.*

Fortune favoured him. In the battle which followed, he was opposed by two generals, Hanno and Bomilcar.

* There is little doubt that this adventure inspired the famous expedition of Regulus in the First Punic War : it revealed once for all the fatal weakness of Carthage—the disaffection of her African subjects.

Whether inspired by Greek example or not, Bomilcar had formed the design of making himself tyrant of Carthage, and imagined that the best way of securing his end was to involve his country in a great disaster, after which he was to come forward as the heaven-appointed deliverer. In the first part of his task he thoroughly succeeded. While Hanno fought with the utmost skill and bravery, Bomilcar deliberately held back his own division; and finally gave orders for its retreat. The natural result was that the army was defeated and driven back upon Carthage.

Apart from the great city herself, few places in her dominions were fortified; and she had never treated her subjects with any sort of consideration. The country was thus an easy prey to the invader, and for some time success crowned his efforts. But he was not really equal to the task; and he had to face not merely determined efforts on the part of the enemy, but mutiny in his own camp, which was suppressed with great difficulty. In this emergency he sent for help to Cyrene, and a large force under Ophellas, one of the officers of Alexander the Great, came to his aid. It would seem as if Agathocles could not live without the excitement of murder. No sooner had the Cyrenæans arrived, than Agathocles, with the usual excuse that Ophellas was conspiring his death, killed him during a conference.

Just at this moment, when there was not unnaturally some confusion among the Greeks, Carthage was in worse confusion; for Bomilcar now made his bid for the tyranny, and began a slaughter of his fellow-citizens closely resembling those which Agathocles had organised

SICILY

in Syracuse. Fortunately the attempt collapsed; the people rallied; Bomilcar was forced to surrender, and duly hanged in the market-place. He had not, however, failed to harm his country. While this struggle was proceeding, it was impossible for Carthage to attack the foreign enemy.

But at this moment Agathocles heard that he was needed at home, where his authority was waning. He returned in haste, leaving the army under the command of his sons. After a short time, during which fortune favoured him, he came back to find his African army, through the incompetence of his sons, on the verge of renewed mutiny, and in utter discouragement. Only a victory could save him. He attacked the Carthaginian camp, and was totally defeated. Nothing remained for him, as for Napoleon in Egypt, but to leave the army to its fate. He secretly embarked on a small boat, and reached Sicily in safety. The army, furious and distracted, killed his two sons, and made terms with Carthage.

Of the further murders, victories, and reverses of the tyrant, there is no need here to speak. He maintained himself in power for several years longer. Finally, feeling his end approaching, he had to consider the problem of the succession. There were two candidates, his nephew, bearing his own name, and his grandson Archagathus. Agathocles chose the nephew; but the grandson seems to have inherited more of his spirit. He invited his uncle to a banquet, spoke him fair, and poisoned him. To dispose of his grandfather he had a ready instrument. Some time before, Agathocles had organised a frightful massacre of the citizens of Egesta.

A beautiful youth named Maenon had seen the slaughter; he had been spared, and had become a favourite slave of the tyrant; but he had never forgotten the horrors he had witnessed. Agatharchus, promising him impunity, sent him to tend Agathocles in his illness; and Maenon poisoned him with a toothpick. Such a " vindex," more contemptible than the ring of Hannibal, might have given inspiration to a Juvenal discoursing on the Vanity of Human Wishes.

With Agathocles we have touched the height and the depth of Greek tyranny; there were many others before and after him, but to tell their story would merely be to add an anticlimax. Even Sparta, which for four hundred years was the very symbol of stable government, fell at last under a savage despot; but Nabis is only a feebler and more despicable Agathocles. The reader has had enough.

To sum up this brief and hasty sketch. The ancient tyrant began by taking advantage of a national emergency, or by inventing such an emergency when it was not obliging enough to exist, and by posing as the one man who could save the State. Having thus gained authority with a show of legality, he slaughtered or banished his enemies. Next, he got rid of possible rivals or dangerous friends. He conciliated religion, or introduced a new one which would support his claims. He blindfolded the people by public works of beauty or utility, which had the incidental advantage of impoverishing them and keeping them busy, so that they had time neither to think nor to conspire. He kept a tight hand on the organs of opinion; induced poets to sing his praises, and suppressed literary works which did not eulogise tyranny. He made, as a rule, alliances with other tyrants, unless they were weak enough to invite attack. If other methods failed, he had recourse to foreign wars, hoping that glory might compensate, in the eyes of his people, for the loss of freedom : and, with a similar view, he competed in the great sacred Pan-hellenic games, success in which brought prestige not merely to the actual contestants, but to the city they represented, and to the man who had trained them and paid their expenses.

Finally, it is noteworthy that, even though the founder of a dynasty may show a certain mildness, yet, if the dynasty manages to last a generation or two, the successors almost invariably deteriorate, until finally they fall as far below their ancestor as Nero below Augustus.

RENAISSANCE ITALY

"Medio de fonte leporum surgit amari aliquid."—*Lucretius.*

It has been truly said that it is impossible to define the Renaissance. We know neither when or why it came about; and its character is a mass of contradictions. The utmost refinement is found alongside the most savage cruelty; religious enthusiasm mingles with paganism or scepticism; delicacy with obscenity. We may content ourselves with saying that it began, roughly, in the time of Petrarch and Boccaccio; that it is marked by an amazing genius in all the arts, poetry, sculpture, painting, and architecture; that it was diligent in searching out and studying the books and other monuments of ancient Greece and Rome; and that, with all this, it was incapable of political stability, and made no progress towards national unity. The wind blows where it lists; there is no explanation of its rise or its fall; and we can but record its speed and the area over which it passes.

The Renaissance age is also the age of the despots: Leonardo and Michael Angelo were contemporaries of the Sforzas and the Medici: and Ariosto was a hanger-on at the court of Ferrara. It was a remarkable age, and among the men of the age the despots were not the least remarkable. When we turn to study these men, we are confronted with the same difficulty as met us in dealing with the Greeks. They are so numerous that a history is impossible, and selection invidious. But the difficulty is all but countervailed by one great advantage. The theory of Italian despotism has been explained once for all by a writer of unique power, whom Bacon eulogised for having described men not as they ought to be or as they like to appear, but as they really are : and from whom so sublime a thinker as Spinoza borrowed the main principles of his political philosophy. Before his book was published, Thomas Cromwell studied it, and urged Reginald Pole to pore over its pages ; and, when it had become widely known, Marlowe and other great dramatists took its hero as a model from which to draw their Tamburlaines and their Richards. I have already referred to the *Prince* of Machiavelli ; and I might, in the present chapter, do little more than translate his more striking paragraphs. In any case, his thoughts will always be present to my mind, and will doubtless constantly recur to the mind of the reader.

In certain cases of Renaissance despotism, not too frequent, we may be reminded of the words of Thucydides about the authority exercised by Pericles in Athens, that the State was in name a republic, but was in actual fact ruled by its first citizen—with this difference, that the rule of Pericles was not permanent ; he founded no dynasty. He might have said when dying, like Mr. Valiant-for-Truth, " I give my courage and skill to him that can get it." Unfortunately, there was no one worthy of the legacy ; and Athens fell into the hands of a crowd of warring demagogues, each trying to outbid the others.

With obvious and natural differences, the career of Cosimo de' Medici has its likenesses to that of Pericles.

In the republic of Florence his father Giovanni had gained great influence by means first of his wealth, which his skill in banking constantly increased, and then his ability as shown in the offices which he never openly sought but to which he was constantly elected. He left, on his death in 1428, a legacy of his possessions and of sound counsel to his two sons Cosimo and Lorenzo. "Accept state-honours," said he, "when they are legally offered: never attempt to seize them." They followed their father's advice. They made no attempt, at first, to alter the constitution; the Council of Ten still remained, and the president, or Gonfaloniere, was still elected every two months. Somehow or other, however, either a Medici or one of the friends of the Medici was always Gonfaloniere, and the Council was always pursuing a Medici policy; but the people hardly noticed it, for the affability and liberality of the great family were always conspicuous: the rich were charmed and the poor relieved. For a short time, indeed, another powerful clan, jealous of the influence thus gained, contrived to seize the rule, and Cosimo had to leave the city; but this was only like the temporary unpopularity of Pericles, which led the citizens of Athens to impose a fine—soon to be regretted. His adversaries were, within a few months, overthrown; Cosimo was invited to return; and thenceforward, to the end of his life, he enjoyed uninterrupted prosperity. It is true that some of his opponents were banished, others put to death (though not, it is said, by Cosimo's orders), and others imprisoned: but such things, we know, had to be after every party victory in Italian cities. They are less horrible than the contemporary savagery of our own Wars of the Roses; and the craft and dexterity—if they be not rather to be called tact—of Cosimo are much less repellent than the treachery and cunning by which Louis XI of France was at the same time making himself the undisputed ruler of his country in the face of ambitious nobles. However we decide to view his authority, it was accepted by the people. Late in life, Cosimo was able to take a further step. He may have doubted whether his son would know how to use the arts which had been so successful when plied by himself. A permanent machinery was desirable. Accordingly, in 1459, Cosimo contrived to have a council of a hundred established, so that, as he put it to a confiding people, the stability of the constitution might be assured. When formed, this council, at any rate as seen by jealous eyes, was found to consist exclusively of Cosimo's adherents.

Cosimo died in 1464, and it was at once seen that his régime had its enemies. An attempt was made, on the part of the exiles and their partisans, to overthrow his son and successor Piero—a conspiracy led by Luca Pitti, the builder of a palace more famous than himself. The conspiracy was foiled by the energy of the young Lorenzo, Piero's son. Piero was either an invalid or a valetudinarian; and we are told that his partisans took advantage of his weakness to indulge in cruelties, peculations, and crimes of all kinds—the usual accompaniments of a rule at once absolute and feeble. But within five years he died, and Lorenzo succeeded, in accordance with the popular desire, to the position which his family had held for so long.

Lorenzo is the very pride and crown of Renaissance

despotism. By his patronage of art and letters, by his own poems, which are far above the ordinary level of princely versifying, and by the use he made of his enormous wealth, he has earned the title of "The Magnificent", and might, had he lived two thousand years before, have served Aristotle as the pattern for his description: "The Magnificent Man is lavish, not for himself, but for the commonwealth; his gifts are as it were dedicatory offerings; it is in his character to arrange his household suitably to his opulence, and to expend rather on the lasting than on the transient, showing greatness in great things, and always in due proportion." And Lorenzo added to magnificence the quality of the Aristotelian Magnanimous Man, who deems himself worthy of great things, being in reality worthy. When all deductions are made, Lorenzo is probably the highest type of his class.

He had dangers to contend with. Like Hippias of Athens, he shared his rule with his brother. Giuliano de' Medici was almost as able as Lorenzo; and both of them, by the vigour of their policy, earned the hatred of Pope Sixtus IV. The result was the famous conspiracy of the Pazzi, engineered by the head of Christianity, and supported by a cardinal, an archbishop, and several less distinguished clergymen, some of whom took an active part in the crime. The Pazzi were a powerful Florentine family, hostile to the Medici, and easy tools for the Pope's purposes. The attempt was made, so as to add every circumstance of horror, in a church, during the most sacred moment of the celebration of Mass, and when Lorenzo had just welcomed the Papal "envoys" to his house. Giuliano was murdered by the Pazzi at the instant when the priest was raising the consecrated wafer. Two priests succeeded in wounding Lorenzo, but failed to complete their work. Meanwhile, the archbishop endeavoured to overthrow the government, and one of the Pazzi, rushing through the streets with the cry of "Liberty", tried to rouse the citizens to revolt. The whole thing was a bloody fiasco. The Pazzi family, so far from gaining even momentary and Rome-propped power, was wiped out; the archbishop was hanged; and the cardinal, clinging like a cowardly Joab to the altar, was saved only by the magnanimity of Lorenzo. As for the murderous priests, they were tracked down by the populace, tortured, and put to death.

Shortly afterwards, Lorenzo heard that a natural son had been born to his brother. He took every care to protect and rear the child, who grew up to be the second Medici Pope, to see Rome sacked by the troops of Charles V, and to be the Clement VII who, by his delays and vacillations, drove Henry VIII to sever England from the Papal obedience.

The aim of Sixtus, in planning this crime, seems to have been neither to restore "liberty", nor to give the rule to the ambitious Pazzi family, but to gain Florence for himself. The attempt was but another instance of the moral confusion caused by the double character of the Popes, who were at the same time the nominal chiefs of Christendom and the overlords of a secular dominion in the "States of the Church"; states which they were ever attempting to enlarge, and the possession of which involved them in innumerable wars, intrigues, and treacheries. The failure of the conspiracy strengthened Lorenzo; and it is to his credit that, unlike Hippias in similar circumstances, he did not become embittered. He did, it is true, show himself utterly pitiless to all who had taken part in the Pazzi rising, and even to those whom he merely suspected of sympathising with it ; and this has led many historians to judge him with extreme severity ; but when he had assured himself that all his dangerous enemies were either dead, or in prison, or exiled, he regained confidence, and with confidence acquired leniency. He was again seen mingling easily with the citizens, and invited people to his house without a sign that he feared he might once more be harbouring assassins. Doubtless he had seen, by the way in which the populace had rallied round him, that his rule had both numerous and enthusiastic supporters. Abroad, also, he found a field more easy to work than before. Sixtus, one of the most turbulent and unscrupulous of all Popes, died ; Italy was able to enjoy something which, in contrast with what had gone before, might be called peace : and peace Lorenzo did all in his power to maintain. He thus had leisure, at last, to devote himself, not merely to the quiet consolidation of his authority, but to the studies, the writings, and the arts which, there is every reason to believe, he really loved, and to the society of the scholars and artists whom he gathered round him. It was he who gave the first encouragement to the genius of Michael Angelo, invited him to the palace, and bade him take a higher room at table. He never forgot his Greek teacher, Marsilio Ficino, and even made an abstract in verse of the Platonic philosophy, based on Marsilio's Latin translation of Plato's Dialogues. The scholar Politian was his intimate friend, and celebrated his Mæcenas with all the fervour of a Horace. When Politian began the long career of the musical drama with his opera *Orfeo*, Lorenzo gave it his princely support. Pulci, another intimate associate, read his *Morgante Maggiore* before Lorenzo as Virgil recited the *Æneid* to Augustus.

I would not pass over in silence this aspect of the Renaissance princedoms, which has almost redeemed their fame, and of which the career of Lorenzo is only the most famous exemplar. Even a condottiere chief, who had turned his arms against the city which had hired his services, did not trust entirely to the sword. By some obscure process the perception penetrated his mind that there were influences more powerful than force, and that, as Napoleon afterwards realised, the " imponderables " have weight. He wished to secure for his throne a sort of legitimacy, and, as he could never attain this by right of birth, he sought it by the encouragement of literature, learning, or art. If rough and uncultured himself, he desired refinement for his children. Thus it would be hard to find a more barbarous or dissolute tyrant than Niccolo d'Este of Ferrara. Yet he put his son Leonello under the tutorship of the great humanist Guarino of Verona; and Leonello became the patron of Mantegna. Printers, engineers, and architects found as munificent supporters in the monarchical cities as in the rich republic of Venice.

But the real dispensers of fame were the teachers and the scholars. A scholar in Italy enjoyed at that time a repute which he has perhaps never had since; for scholarship, in addition to its other attractions, was then a novelty, and like so many novelties became a fashion. This was a repetition of the capture of republican Rome by captive Greece; an invasion which came in like a flood. Padua went wild when it imagined it had found the tomb of Livy. A Poggio, bringing to light the lost Institutes of Quintilian, or the Annals of Tacitus, was as famous as, a few years later, Columbus became by the discovery of the New World—and better treated by his beneficiaries: while Chalcondylas and Argyropoulos the exiles enjoyed in Florence and elsewhere the prestige of Imperial ambassadors. Even in England Humphrey of Gloucester and the savage Lancastrian, John Tiptoft of Worcester, added to the splendour of their rank by their learning and patronage of learning: and Tiptoft's elegant Latinity "drew tears from the eyes of Pope Pius II himself." Those who wished to be in fashion, therefore, if they could not be scholars themselves, made friends of scholars, and hoped to share their glory. All remember the almost pleading tone of the letter of Augustus to Horace, gently complaining that he had not seen his name in the poet's works, and hinting that even an Emperor's renown might lose lustre by the omission. Very similar are the letters of Italian despots, fourteen centuries later, to literary men; and the independence of the answers is like Horace's sense of a dominion in his own sphere as all but equal to Cæsar's in another. No illustration of this could be more striking than the story of the intercourse between the great humanist Vittorino of Feltre and Gonzaga of Mantua, which is so admirably recounted by Dr. Woodward in his life of Vittorino.

Luigi Gonzaga had made himself, by the usual methods, first captain-general of Mantua, and then tyrant, as early as 1328; and his dynasty lasted till 1708. His descendant Gianfrancesco, now exalted to a Marquisate, was, says Woodward, on the whole a favourable representative of the type of condottiere prince. To his people he showed himself a "benevolent" ruler; he kept on good terms with the Church, maintained friendly relations with the despots of Milan and Ferrara, married a daughter of the great house of Malatesta, and faithfully earned the pay of the republic of Venice by serving in its wars, which Venice always preferred to carry on by mercenary aid. "His assassinations were not obtrusive"; and though, in the common despotic fashion, he was alienated for years from his eldest son, he finally became reconciled and restored the youth to favour.

"Virtue", in the Renaissance sense, he had in plenty; but he needed "glory"; and glory could be gained only by association with poets, architects, painters, or scholars. At that time the scholars had the preference. The Visconti courted Chrysoloras as the d'Estes courted Guarino. If Gonzaga was to rival these, he must seek another scholar whose presence would lend lustre to his court, and who would give an education to his children which would mean that the tradition of culture and refinement would be handed down to future generations. As, later, the Duke of Suffolk secured Roger Ascham as the tutor of his daughter Lady Jane Grey, so the Marquis looked round for a famous teacher for his family. He applied first to Guarino; but Guarino was pledged to the Visconti as professor of rhetoric. As an educator, Guarino had but one competitor, Vittorino, who was then the master of a school in Venice. It was not easy to obtain Vittorino's consent; he was, he said, happy in his post, and had no wish to remove ; he was not attracted by the life of courts, he loved peace and feared the jealousy the offered place was sure to arouse, and he had no love of show. But the Marquis was not deterred; he allowed the humanist to fix his own salary, and urged, as a special inducement, his anxiety to give the best education to his children. Vittorino was at last persuaded, seeing that to train up these children in the way they should go might be for the benefit not only of the Mantuan citizens, but also of the towns into whose ruling families the daughters might marry. "I accept the post," said he, "but on this condition only, that you shall require of me nothing unworthy of either of us ; and I will contrive to serve you so long as your life shall command respect." Gonzaga took no offence ; and Vittorino stayed in the service of the family till he died twenty-three years later.

Nothing more charming than the picture of that service —provided we withdraw our gaze from the darker background—can easily be discovered in history. The school, to which came not only the Gonzaga children, but those of great scholars like Filelfo and of many princes, was cheerful, happy, and serene. Vittorino had a large staff of masters, who caught his spirit ; and the place was informed with the enthusiasm of humanism, of religion, and of noble ambition. "I remember," says a contemporary, "that Vittorino, now well advanced in years, would of a winter's morning come early, candle in one hand and book in the other, and rouse a pupil in whose progress he was specially interested ; he would leave him time to dress, waiting patiently till he was ready ; then he would hand him over the book, and encourage him with grave and earnest words to high endeavour."

Nor was it only on the "book" that Vittorino concentrated his attention. Like Milton after him, he believed in the training of the body; his pupils were exercised in out-door games, and specially in fencing. As many of them were to be soldiers, this was natural; but the equal cultivation of mind and body was of the essence of the Humanist ideal. Provided that athleticism was not carried too far, Vittorino encouraged athletics; but he held the old Roman view that a gentleman was degraded if he gained the skill of a professional. If small boys talked of their lessons out of school, Vittorino turned them into the field to play; but he never allowed thoughts of play to spoil working hours.

Due exceptions being made, Vittorino gave the same education to girls as to boys; and the daughters of the nobles who came to his school left it with as high a culture as the sons. Here, as in so many other ways, Vittorino was in advance of his age.

But the point to notice is that in all this the master was supported by the Marquis. The school-house, The Joyous or The Jocose, for both names were used, was provided by the prince, and the wide meadows and playing fields were kept in order at his expense. No difference was permitted in the treatment of scholars of varying rank; the Gonzaga children were, by the direction of their father, kept on the same level as a lad too poor to pay fees; and the princess Cecilia learnt like other girls. Here the Marchioness, who was as keenly interested in the school as her husband, was of great use to the master.

This, of course, illustrates the best side of despotism, precisely as the beautiful culture of certain rich English houses illustrates the best side of wealth ; and we all know how much easier it is for Universities or other great institutions to gain help from one or two millionaires than to extract equivalent benefit from the small contributions of multitudes. The conduct of Gonzaga, and of others like him, reveals one great advantage which single rule has over the rule of many ; undertakings may be carried through speedily and effectively which would take committees much time and tiresome deliberation. Whether such amenities are in the long run worth the price is another question ; but it is certain that one reason why despotisms have been welcomed is that people have wearied of the tardiness and other vexatious defects inseparable from democratic constitutions.

To return from Mantua to Florence. Whatever we may think of Lorenzo—and there have been many writers who have refused to be dazzled by his magnificence or to be deceived by the eulogies of his flatterers—he could not pass on his qualities to his descendants. Like his father, Cosimo, he left his son Piero good advice : " Never forget that you are only a citizen of Florence " : and Piero at once disobeyed it. In his determination to make himself more than a citizen, a purpose which he could not carry out without foreign aid, he applied for help to the King of Naples, a tyrant in all but name. As it was clear that an alliance between two such powers would be dangerous to other despots, the ruler of Milan, Lodovico Sforza, conceived the desperate idea of calling in the aid of Charles VIII of France ; and the result was the famous expedition of 1494, in which the French encountered so little resistance that, as Bacon said, they made their way not with the sword but with the chalk with which the soldiers marked the houses where they meant to lodge. Piero's terror was abject. He threw himself at Charles's feet, and offered him three cities and a fortress, in return for the promise that Florence should be spared. Charles looked on him with contempt; but the Florentines were more contemptuous still. When Piero returned to the city he found the people so hostile that he thought it desirable to retire to Venice: and Florence, for a few years, became a theocracy under the domination of Savonarola. Piero made an attempt to regain his power; but the only result was that his partisans were captured and the leaders put to death. He never returned. After a series of humiliating requests for aid to all sorts of people, who flattered and betrayed him, he at last attached himself to Louis XII of France, and perished in the great defeat of the Garigliano which Louis suffered at the hands of the Spaniards. His cruelties and follies had lost him his great inheritance. There will be few to sympathise with his misfortunes; for the man who, in pursuit of personal power, seeks help from foreign rulers, and endeavours to purchase it by surrendering portions of his country's territory, has, till very recent times, failed to gain wide approval. Even a sonnet or two, in which Piero asserts, in due octave and sestet form, his love of Florence, can hardly convince us that his love was pure and unselfish.

After the death of Piero, his family made a successful effort to return. Florence, then guided by Piero Soderini, was again weak; Soderini's character is sufficiently shown by the famous epigram of Machiavelli, which denies him after death the honour of damnation, and consigns him to the limbo of babies. The two brothers of Piero, Cardinal Giovanni and Giuliano, collected an armed force from all quarters, and attacked the city. Soderini made a feeble resistance, and the Medici entered in triumph. Shortly afterwards the Pope died, and the Cardinal was elected in his place, to become eternally remembered as Leo X. This, of course, meant a great increase of strength to the Medici family. Giuliano soon died, and the Pope made his nephew Lorenzo the ruler of Florence. Lorenzo marks an even lower stage of tyranny than Piero. His character was bad, his administration oppressive, and his foreign policy distinguished solely by an attack upon the city of Urbino, of which the Pope, regardless of justice, made him duke. He will, however, always be remembered as the father of Catherine dei Medici, Queen of France, and author of the Massacre of St. Bartholomew. He died soon after her birth; and the direct line came to an end. Alessandro, supposed to be his natural son, but really in all probability, the son of the second Medici Pope Clement VII, succeeded to the rule; and in the lowest deep a lower deep was found. Alessandro was Tarquin the Proud and his son Sextus in one; no Oriental sultan, born in the purple, was ever more rapacious, licentious, or contemptible. Vengeance came, as in the case of the Tarquins, from within the tyrant's own family. His cousin Lorenzino murdered him in his bed, pretending to be the Brutus restoring liberty, but really aiming at the tyranny himself. He did not gain his end. His peregrinations through the city, with the cry, " Liberty, freedom,

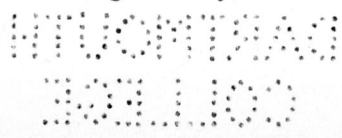

tyranny is dead ", made no impression on the people, who, though not particularly shocked by the crime, did not expect much from its perpetrator. The exiles who had fled from the cruelties of Alessandro assembled troops, and advanced towards Florence. They showed little intention of allying themselves with Lorenzino, who wisely disappeared, and did not think himself safe till he reached Turkey. It looked for a moment as if some sort of republic might be restored. But a mightier power intervened. The Emperor Charles V did not desire to have republicans near Rome as well as Protestants in Germany. He therefore supported the cause of yet another Medici, the youthful Cosimo, of a distant branch of the family. With such aid Cosimo was easily victorious; the exiles were defeated; large numbers were put to death; others thrown into dungeons; some killed themselves. After these exploits, Cosimo assumed the title of Grand Duke; and the once turbulent Florentines sank into an apathy which remained unbroken for two centuries. The Grand Dukes shared in the general decline, and gradually degenerated until they passed almost unnoticed from the world.

No account of the Italian tyrants could be complete without some reference to Cæsar Borgia, who is in a sense the hero of Machiavelli's *Prince*. His career is interesting chiefly as showing how princedoms were obtained; for by a combination of ill-fortune and his own folly he was unable to keep what he won. His father, Pope Alexander VI, has the worst reputation of all the Popes; but probably unjustly. It is true that he gained his election by unblushing bribery, and that his morals were conspicuously bad even in a loose age : his nepotism was no better than that of his predecessors ; he was shifty, hasty, and imprudent. But the secret poisonings and other detestable crimes imputed to him by contemporaries and by later historians are, with perhaps a few exceptions, in all likelihood legendary. Even to the death of Savonarola, for which he has been so severely condemned, he was driven only by a series of provocations which less placable Popes would have punished much more promptly. His fatal fault was his family ambition. He was anxious to provide permanent principalities for his sons, and a splendid marriage, or, if necessary, splendid marriages, for his daughter Lucretia. As, however, the grant of a principality in the States of the Church might be annulled by his successor, he wished his sons to make themselves so strong that to depose them would be impossible. His plans for his elder son, the Duke of Gandia, came to nothing : for the Duke was the victim of a mysterious murder, which has provided a theme for historians, novelists, poets, and guessers ever since. The father's grief was keen ; for some time he even repented of his sins, and became a reformed character. But the offending Adam soon returned. His younger son, Cæsar, remained to be his evil genius. Cæsar had been a cardinal ; but a Church career did not suit his ambition. He threw aside the hat, and set to work to become a prince of a secular state. It is now that his peculiar talents show themselves. By craft, trickery, murder ; by the dexterous use of the Papal religious powers, which still had some effect ; by promises which he kept as long as to keep them was to his advantage ; by personal charm which he well knew how to use when it was desirable, he conquered one by one the petty rulers of the Romagna, who were nominally tributaries of the Pope, and who could therefore be easily accused of insubordination or treason. Once ruler, he acted according to the maxim afterwards expounded by Machiavelli, and ceased his cruelties—for the same reason that had induced him to practise them. Not for long had the Romagnese enjoyed so just and beneficent a despotism; and Cæsar was remembered with gratitude for years after his death. An attack on Urbino had less justification: the Duke was benevolent and popular: but it was equally successful.

These victories enabled Cæsar to call to his aid a number of the condottieri soldiers who were willing to serve any commander who could give them the hope of loot; and it is at this point that we meet an incident which has been immortalised by Machiavelli, and which throws a vivid light on the character of the tyrannies of that time.

Oliverotto of Fermo, left orphaned, was brought up kindly by his uncle Giovanni Fogliani. In early days he served under the soldier of fortune, Pavolo Vitelli, and gained great repute as a good officer. When Pavolo died, he continued to serve under his brother Vitellozzo. But later, despising equality with others, he determined with the aid of Vitelli and of certain discontented citizens of Fermo, to make himself master of the city. He wrote therefore to his uncle, saying that he desired to revisit his native place; and, to show that he had not spent his time in vain, requested that he might be allowed to come with a hundred men: he would thus honour the city in honouring himself. Once received, he invited his uncle and other leading men to a banquet, and murdered them all—a deed which Machiavelli compares with that by which Agathocles made himself tyrant of Syracuse. Oliverotto retained his tyranny for a year, and might, says Machiavelli, have rivalled Agathocles but for a single mistake. Along with other captains, he hired himself out to Cæsar Borgia. But mercenaries are not always reliable. When Cæsar was planning vast schemes of further conquest, including the capture of Florence, he discovered that the captains were intriguing with his enemies. He acted with his usual skill. He summoned them to a conference, talked with them in a friendly fashion, and —with an *arriere pensée*—reconciled them to himself. With their help he captured Sinigaglia; and then, having no further use for them, inveigled them into a snare, and strangled them all. Among the victims were Vitelli and Oliverotto.

Meanwhile, the great families of the Colonna and the Orsini, which in Rome itself were the chief enemies of the Pope, were crushed; and it seemed not impossible that Alexander and Cæsar might form a dominion which should be the nucleus of a united Italy. Whatever their purposes, they suddenly came to naught. The Pope died, it was widely believed of poison meant for a guest; and it happened that Cæsar fell ill simultaneously. " I was ready for everything," said Cæsar afterwards to Machiavelli, " except that I might be disabled by illness when my father died."

Sick as he was, he gained possession of the treasures in the Vatican, but failed to seize the Castle of St. Angelo. A new Pope had to be elected. Alexander had crowded the College with Spanish Cardinals, in order to secure a continuation of his policy; but they did not act as he hoped. They chose first a mild and upright invalid, Pius III; and when Pius died within a month they proceeded again to an election. The most likely candidate was Cardinal delle Rovere; and Cæsar thought it the safest plan to bargain with the Cardinal. On condition that he was made Gonfaloniere of the Church, Cæsar would secure the Papacy for delle Rovere. It has often been remarked that men who invariably deceive others constantly fancy that others will not deceive them. The new Pope, who took the ominous name of Julius II, was a deadly enemy of the Borgias. No sooner was he chosen than he threw Cæsar into prison, deprived him of all the cities and castles he had won, and finally dismissed him to be arrested by the Spanish King of Naples. The King despatched him to Spain, where he contrived to escape from confinement, but a year or two later perished in a battle in Navarre. Like Oliverotto, he had made one mistake, and that a fatal one. As Machiavelli sums up the case: "Considering all the Duke's actions (Cæsar had been given by Louis XII the dukedom of Valentinois) he can hardly be severely censured: I would rather recommend him for imitation to all those who by fortune or by the arms of others have attained to rule. For, with his great soul and lofty aims, it was impossible for him to govern otherwise; and nothing prevented his reaching his ends but the shortness of Alexander's life and his own illness. Anyone, therefore, who desires, in the infancy of his principate, to assure himself against enemies, to acquire friends, to conquer whether by force or by fraud, to make himself loved or feared by the populace, to win the devotion of his soldiers, to crush those who can or may oppose him, to put new life into old forms, to be severe or gracious, magnanimous and liberal, to put down mutineers in his forces and form new armies, to keep up friendships with kings and other princes, such a man can find no better model than Cæsar Borgia. He is censurable for nothing but the election of Julius II. He may not have had the power to choose a Pope to his liking; but he could always have prevented the choice of a Pope he disliked: and he should never have consented to the election of any Cardinal whom he had offended, or who, on becoming Pope, might have reason to fear him. He ought to have created a Spaniard Pope, or failing him, one of his Italian friends. A man who fancies that in great personages later benefits wipe out the memory of former injuries, deceives himself. Cæsar, therefore, erred in supporting Julius; and this error was the cause of his ruin."

If we inquire why this man, so unscrupulous and so ruthless, came so near success, we see at once that circumstances favoured him. At the time when he arose, Italy was in a state of distraction, and there was hardly a town, outside of Venetia, which did not, in miniature, show the distractions of the whole peninsula. In the north, Lodovico Sforza, by summoning Charles VIII into Italy, had revived the antiquated claims of France to Milan, and suggested to the ambitious Louis XII designs on the whole country. In Florence, as we have seen, there was confusion enough. In the south, Spain was gradually making herself mistress of the kingdom of Naples. In Italy itself there was nothing to oppose to all this but the

Papal power; and that, feeble as it was at best, was hampered by warring factions in Rome, and by the very dubious loyalty of the rulers of the cities in the States of the Church. These rulers, for the most part, were tyrannical, stupid, and detested by their subjects. A man, therefore, who appeared as the saviour of the citizens, would not be harshly criticised by them if his methods of getting rid of their tyrants were somewhat drastic or perfidious. The end would justify the means. When this was accomplished, Cæsar's designs, so far as we can see, took a wider sweep. He aimed at nothing less than a united Italy. Of the two great countries, he meant to use France, first, to conquer Florence, and then to expel the Spaniards. After that, we may guess with some probability, he would have watched his opportunity, formed a Holy League like that which Julius contrived later, and thrust the French in their turn out of Italy. A plan like this it was that commended Cæsar to such men as Machiavelli, who were sick of seeing their country at the mercy of foreigners, and would pardon any man, whatever his crimes, who banished the hated alien, and incidentally crushed the petty tyrants. Italy had to wait for three centuries before a man as crafty, and as able, as Cæsar arose to do the work. Nor was Cavour much more scrupulous, though more successful, than the Borgia. He, too, called in French aid, and utilised it for his own purposes. He, too, used perfidy and craft, when desirable, without hesitation. And he too thought the end justified the means. "If," said he, "we did for ourselves what we do for our country, what scoundrels we should be."

NAPOLEON

"Let no one wonder that, in speaking of principates, I adduce the greatest examples: for men must almost always walk in paths beaten by others, and their deeds are imitations. If then you are not able to keep precisely to these beaten paths, nor to attain to the stature of the men you imitate, none the less you will, if wise, always *begin* as the great men have begun before you, in order that, though you cannot rival their full excellence, you may at least achieve some shadow of it."—*Machiavelli*.

I AM not about to add one more to the fifty thousand volumes which have been written on Napoleon. Every word he spoke, every line he wrote, every battle he fought, has been sufficiently discussed, from every point of view, and will be discussed again. What I propose to do is, in a very few lines, to consider him as a despot—though the despotism is only one aspect of his infinite variety. And this for two reasons. First, as Napoleon was a student of history, and not least of Plutarch, he must have pondered over the careers of ancient autocrats, and must have had them before his mind as models for his own path to autocracy. He learned generalship from Hannibal, and tyranny from Dionysius. Secondly, he has in his turn become a model. I do not think that the Hitlers, Mussolinis, Kemals, or the soldiers who have recently set up a military rule in Iraq, have troubled much about Agathocles or Peisistratus; but they have all had Napoleon in view. As we shall see, a very determined South American Dictator deliberately and openly fashioned himself after the great Corsican. The German military caste read and re-read the campaigns of 1796 and 1814 as patterns of the art of war, and would-be dictators have studied the means by which Napoleon gained his power, maintained it, and lost it, in order to read in the story at once an example and a warning. It cannot therefore be irrelevant to sketch, very briefly, this aspect of a myriad-minded man.

How many changes of government France had endured between the beginning of the Revolution in 1789 and 1796 when Bonaparte began to be really famous, we may leave to the arithmetical historians to count. At the time of Bonaparte's rise to fame she was under the Directory, a corrupt junta which could make neither war nor peace, and was unequal both to keeping order at home and to gaining success abroad. Its one honest member was Carnot, the " organiser of victory ", who was however fatally hampered by his connection with the Reign of Terror. The chief man was Barras, who used his position to fill his pockets. It was this government which appointed Bonaparte to his Italian command. He had taken its measure before he left France, and his contempt for it was hardly disguised when success came to his arms. We might call him already a despot when, in total disregard of the wishes of his nominal chiefs, he made treaties, set up republics, and annexed principalities. We might put the date even earlier, at the moment when Masséna, after a brief interview with him, remarked, "We have met our master." He returned victorious in 1797, and the Directors at once saw in him a pressing danger. They tried to get rid of him by offering him the thankless post of General of the Army of England ; but he saw the snare, and took no notice. Even then he pondered the design of overthrowing the Government; but his keen eye detected that the pear was not ripe. Instead, he set out on his Egyptian expedition, the object of which was manifold. It was precisely the grandiose and romantic adventure which would appeal to the masses; but also it would touch England in her most sensitive point by the threat to India, and it might enable France to see what would happen when he, the chosen hero, was absent. Nothing could have suited him better than what *did* happen. A new coalition was formed against the Republic, and was everywhere successful. Bonaparte's Italian conquests were nearly all lost; the general who, the Directors hoped, would eclipse his glory was defeated and killed at Novi; the buffer-states of Switzerland were in danger; and Austria had largely recovered her lost prestige. At home there was poverty, distress, and discontent; the Jacobins were once more becoming noisy, and a new Reign of Terror seemed imminent.

At this crisis, the Abbé Sieyès, whose famous pamphlet, "What is the Third Estate?" had been the herald of the Revolution, and whose fertile mind had produced constitutions as a conjurer brings rabbits out of a hat, emerged from obscurity. He had, as he said, done wonders in the Terror; he had stayed alive. He now appeared with another constitution in his pocket, and the cry went up all over the country that the corrupt rulers must be deposed. One *coup d'état* with that purpose was actually tried, and failed; another was only the more plainly necessary.

Bonaparte, watching all this from Egypt, determined

not to omit the tide in his affairs, but to take it at the flood. He left his army to look after itself, and with a few friends embarked for France. By Cæsarean good-fortune he eluded the British cruisers, and landed at Fréjus in the nick of time. His glamorous Oriental enterprise had already filled the ears of men; and his return was like an Avatar. He knew how to utilise the moment. " I left France," said he, " prosperous and peaceful at home and victorious abroad; I come back to find her vanquished abroad and at home in utter confusion and misery." It was a bid for confidence; and the people at once, informally but decisively, owned their deliverer. His journey to Paris was a triumphal progress; his reception there was wildly enthusiastic. The street in which he lodged was renamed the Rue de la Victoire, and was daily crowded with visitors and sightseers. Among these was Sieyès, who had long been looking for a soldier who was also a statesman, or for a statesman who was also a soldier. Two years before, Hoche, who might, possibly, have filled the bill, had died. There was one other soldier, and only one, Moreau, with some sort of statesmanlike ability. But Moreau knew his own limitations. " There," he said to Sieyès, " *there* is your man for the new *coup d'état.*" Sieyès looked, and at once entered into an alliance with the soldier-statesman, in order by his means to establish, at last, the perfect constitution, in which Bonaparte was to act and Sieyès to advise. The hero listened, and perceived that the " idealogue " would be useful: but meanwhile he was receiving, flattering, and winning over by promises —often mutually destructive—representatives of every party. He drugged the Royalists with hints that he might restore the Bourbons, the Jacobins with eulogies of Robespierre, the theorists with talk on political liberty, and everybody with hopes of peace and general improvement. The result was the revolution of the 18th Brumaire —November 1799; a badly managed business which nearly failed, strangely enough, through Napoleon's own vacillation and timidity, but which was saved by the extraordinary tenacity and daring of his brother Lucien and by the courage of Sieyès, who, wishing to keep alive through yet another revolution, urged the soldier on to soldierly vigour. From that moment there was no fear. The Assembly put Napoleon out of the law; he retorted by putting it out of the Chamber. A personal assault on him, and a slight scratch on his hand, were exactly what he required. "Assassins," he cried, "the hirelings of perfidious Albion, had attacked the saviour of France with daggers." This Peisistratus touch was enough. Within a few hours the Directory was, to all intents and purposes, overthrown, and that—apart from the scratch—without the shedding of a drop of blood; and a provisional Government was formed, with Bonaparte, Sieyès, and a nonentity named Ducos, as joint Consuls. All three swore a solemn oath of fidelity to the Republic one and indivisible, promising to maintain liberty, equality and representative government. The change was welcomed by almost the whole country; Bonaparte was expected to be the saviour of France from Jacobinism within and from the Coalition without. This constitution lasted six weeks and three days. At the end of that time Sieyes and Ducos retired, and Bonaperte remained First Consul, with two new colleagues, who counted for nothing. A Senate, largely composed of *savants*, was nominated by Sieyès, and a Lower House was formed out of men who had served in various posts since 1789. The real administration was in the hands of a small Council of State, which never met as a body. Bonaparte, to prevent its members from becoming too important, always met them separately. They soon became not colleagues, but servants. Berthier, one of the worst of generals and one of the greatest of Chiefs of the Staff, and Maret, a civilian Berthier, were the most trusted. Two men of first-rate ability, Talleyrand and Fouché, Prefect in effective control of the police, for the present concealed their capacity, and served with the rest. The first task of Fouché was to suppress more than sixty out of seventy-six Parisian newspapers ; a little later a censorship of the theatres was set up by decree. Nothing was to be known, and no opinions were to be publicly uttered, which did not suit the First Consul.

The country, on the whole, accepted all this, on one condition, that the war should be brought to a satisfactory end. So far, Bonaparte's aim was to conciliate all parties. The Royalists waited daily for his appearance as the General Monk of a Bourbon Restoration ; the Jacobins expected a more popular constitution ; and no one was openly repulsed apart from the armed Chouans of the North-West. But a policy of this kind means that the extremists of every party will in time be dissatisfied : and it was imperative to win a victory. The victory came at Marengo, in June 1800, when Bonaparte crushed the Austrians in Italy, and in December at Hohenlinden, when Moreau utterly defeated them in Germany. Peace with Austria followed in 1801. England alone remained, and at Amiens, early in 1802, peace was made with her also. By these treaties France obtained the Rhine boundary, and was practically mistress besides of Holland, the western principalities of Germany, Switzerland, and the whole of Northern Italy. What Louis XIV, in fifty years, had failed to accomplish, the Republic had more than accomplished in a decade. Bonaparte, the chief agent in this astonishing result, was naturally all but a demigod. Sixty years later, one of Napoleon III's deadliest enemies said, " I will forgive him everything if he gives us back the Rhine frontier." Napoleon III's uncle had, in 1802, given France more than the Rhine frontier; and thousands of his enemies not only forgave him, but adored him.

The republic, nominally, still existed. It was therefore desirable so to manage the Senate that further advance might be made in apparent adherence to the Constitution. As soon, therefore, as the Peace of Amiens was concluded, a proposal was made that *Napoleon* Bonaparte (note the use of the Christian name) should be made First Consul for life: and when the Senate gave him the office only for an additional ten years, he made no overt objection: but proceeded to submit the question to a *plébiscite* or vote of the whole nation. There were regiments in the army which might prove troublesome, as the army of Cromwell had prevented Oliver from becoming King. These were shipped off to perish of fever in St. Domingo. Other soldiers were flattered by the establishment of the Legion of Honour, by monetary and other rewards, or by provision for sickness and disablement.

Nevertheless, many of the chief generals were opposed

to Bonaparte's obvious designs, and an obscure plot was formed for checkmating him. Here he acted with caution. He publicly announced that the generals were trying to subject France to military domination; "and that," he said, "we will never permit." An arrest or two followed on the pretence that his life had been aimed at; and the generals were quietly scattered about the country. The *plébiscite* was then held, and he was accepted by the people as First Consul for life by a majority of three and a half millions against eight thousand. The Senate then gave him the right of appointing his successor.

Already three or four conspiracies, real or pretended, had been "discovered" by the police. One was attributed to the Jacobins, and was used to get rid of their remaining leaders. Another, organised by the Royalists, was unquestionably genuine; an infernal machine killed several people, but Bonaparte escaped. This incident immensely increased his popularity.

Some months later, another conspiracy was "discovered", genuine in the sense that Bonaparte's removal was intended. But the conspirators, most of whom were Royalists, were urged on by Fouché, who hoped, by unearthing their plots, to earn favour with the First Consul. The chiefs were Cadoudal, a Royalist, Pichegru, a former Republican general, and the Polignacs, a fanatical Bourbonist family. Attempts were made to induce Moreau, a strong republican, to join, but utterly failed. The remarkable fact is that Fouché, though he was behind the whole movement, did not know its ramifications, and for a time the police were quite at a loss. Gradually more and more came to light; it appeared that the conspirators were expecting a Bourbon prince to arrive at the critical moment. The police waited, in the hope that he might actually arrive. But it was not in the nature of the Bourbons to run risks. Pichegru and Cadoudal were therefore arrested and with them Moreau, the Polignacs, and several others. Pichegru died in prison; how, whether by suicide or murder, no one knows. Cadoudal and about twenty others were subjected to a very harsh form of "third degree," and were finally condemned. Among these was Moreau, whom there was a very strong desire to compromise, as his great reputation, and honest Republicanism, made him still a dangerous rival. It required little less than main force to induce the judges to condemn him; but at last their consent was extorted, and he was sentenced to two years' imprisonment. Eventually, Bonaparte agreed to pardon him, and he was allowed to sail for America. The First Consul had now no serious competitor; Moreau lived peacefully in America, until, after Napoleon's Russian disaster, he was induced to join the Allies, and fell in the great battle of Dresden.

But more was to result from this conspiracy than even the removal of Moreau. To throw terror into the hearts of the Royalists, Bonaparte, unable to seize any of the princes who had actually conspired, arrested, on neutral territory, the Duke of Enghien, a Bourbon who had had nothing to do with the plot, hurried him across the border, and after a mock-trial, had him shot at dead of night. Things now rapidly tended to the great consummation. The few papers that were still allowed to appear were full of invectives against the Royal assassins who had striven to compass the death of the hero who alone stood between France and destruction; and the cry, skilfully engineered and kept up, was everywhere raised that he should "make his work, like his glory, immortal." A month after the murder of the Duke, the Senate presented an address in which, with some ambiguity, it was hinted that the First Consul should become hereditary Emperor, and that thus, even if assassins should succeed in their atrocious plans, the dynasty would be secure. He answered, "Explain yourselves more fully": and they replied, "Reason, glory, and gratitude all unite to demand that Napoleon be hereditary Emperor." This was in April 1804. In December, in the presence of the Pope, he crowned himself.

It is idle to assert that during the Consulate, Napoleon did not confer enormous benefits on his country. There is hardly a parallel in history to the superhuman energy with which he suppressed disturbances, abolished abuses, and turned chaos into order. The words of Milton on the Creation have been, not inappropriately, applied to his work,

"Confusion heard his voice, and wild uproar stood ruled."

Even Julius Cæsar, in this respect, cannot compare with him. But there was one fatal defect. The work, great and beneficent as it was, was done primarily for himself, and only secondly for France. So long as his own interest and that of his country coincided, it was a magnificent achievement. When they began to diverge, it ceased to be useful, and gradually became disastrous. The inevitable degradation set in. Ambition grew by what it was fed on—foreign conquest took the place of defence, and every conquest led to further aggressions, until he himself could not have told what were his real designs. At last his very marshals wearied of war; the dying Lannes urged him, in vain, to cease from fighting; Talleyrand, to no purpose, begged him not to attack Spain. Finally, the saviour of France was discovered to have worn her to a shadow, and it was with relief that she received those armies as conquerors which, twenty years before, she had risen to repel.

SOUTH AMERICA

" Even if we decide that monarchical rule is the best, what of the King's children ? If the sons are no better than they often are, the State suffers."—*Aristotle*.

Dictatorships follow revolutions ; and in no country have revolutions been more frequent or more far-reaching than in South America. One great revolution, which occurred in the twenties of the nineteenth century, ended in the destruction of the Spanish dominion : and left behind a legacy of anarchy. In place of an incompetent and detested rule, there sprang up a multitude of quarrelling despots, hardly to be distinguished from highwaymen. Corruption and chicanery were rampant in the so-called lawcourts, justice was not to be obtained, chance, fraud, or force decided every question. Any man who could gather around him a band of attached followers, whom he could reward with loot, might look forward to a period of brigand-ascendancy, until a stronger than he came, and in turn assumed a tyranny like that of the king-priest of Aricia—" the priest who slew the slayer, and should himself be slain." At times, indeed, there rose a man who, by superlative ability, ruthlessness, and craft, maintained himself in power for a score of years ; and of this class I know no better type than Rodriguez Francia, Dictator of Paraguay from 1814 to 1840.

Dr. Francia will be remembered longer than most as having attracted the notice of Carlyle, to whom he appeared as one of his favourite Heroes or Strong Men. In his detestation of Parliamentary government, and what he called "twaddle in Exeter-hall or elsewhere," Carlyle was always ready to hold up for admiration some man who had contrived to compel a people to obey his single will; and this feeling led him at times into strange vagaries: it made him write ten volumes on Frederick the Great and devote fifty pages to eulogy of so poor a creature as Governor Eyre. In Dr. Francia he fancied he had found another specimen of the genus—a hero who would shoot down all opposition, but who, strangely enough, would show no inclination to shoot Carlyle himself. He would, in fact, be a despot following his own ideas, and yet somehow be discovered to be following the lead of the Sage of Chelsea.

Francia was born in 1757, the son of a cattle-breeder near Asuncion. His father, wishing him to become a priest, sent him to the University of Cordova, where he seems to have learnt some mathematics, and enough French to read the Encyclopædists and to decide that the Church was not for him. He turned to the law, and became distinguished as one of the few incorruptible advocates in the whole of Paraguay. He was known as gloomy, forceful, honest, and a student—his library consisted of no fewer than three hundred volumes—and it is not surprising either that he should have been chosen secretary to the Government, or that he should have been disgusted with the ignorance, venality, and loquacity of his colleagues. In 1813, by some manœuvring which is not clearly described, he managed to have himself and a certain Fulgencio declared joint consuls—doubtless in imitation of Napoleon, of whom we know him to have been an admirer. During the following year he must have been vigorously working, especially among the soldiery; for at the next Congress we find Fulgencio quietly pushed out of the way, and Francia proclaimed Dictator for three years. It is said that the members were drunk when they gave their decisive vote. Some months later, with suspicious unanimity, the three years were enlarged into " the duration ".

From that moment he held the power and used it. The army was well-drilled and well-paid, Francia, amid his multitudinous other activities, himself taking part in the exercises, and sometimes personally teaching the recruits to shoot with the rifle. Guards were set along the borders of the country to prevent the inroads of Indians, possible aspirants to the Dictatorship, and traders. For Francia was resolved to make Paraguay absolutely self-contained and self-sufficient, and allowed neither imports nor exports—except the imports of arms and the exports to pay for them. All other foreign trade was under the most rigid restrictions; licences were hard to obtain, and were given only for heavy payments which greatly helped the revenues. It would be difficult to find in all history an example of nationalism—which Francia called patriotism—carried to such lengths as this. Needless to add that among the goods excluded were books—for there was no knowing what subversive doctrines a book might contain.

For opponents of the régime there was short shrift; and, as so often, it was old colleagues who became opponents and were put out of the way. Fulgencio started a conspiracy, and got no further than the start. A letter was intercepted; Francia moved with the speed of lightning. In a few hours Fulgencio was captured and shot. On nine successive days, eight others of the ringleaders, or suspected ringleaders (for suspicion was enough) were similarly put to death. From that moment began a reign of terror; prisoners were tortured and forced to confess whatever suited the Dictator; three hundred were thrown into dungeons where such as survived the horrors were broken in spirit. After eighteen months these victims were released—on payment of fines amounting in all to 150,000 pesos. And, for the rest of Francia's reign, massacres occurred at irregular intervals to revive the requisite terror in the people.

Though Francia had little religion, he seems to have resolved to make Paraguay another Tibet, with himself as Grand Lama. Not only could no foreigner enter the country, but no foreigner who happened to be in it was allowed to leave. One unlucky Frenchman tried to escape; he was captured and brought back. He tried again; he was again taken, and this time shot. The illustrious Liberator Bolivar endeavoured to induce the Dictator to give Paraguay its proper place as a South American State. Francia replied that Paraguay could get along very well as it was. Brazil—then a Portuguese kingdom, sent a consul to Asuncion. The consul, unable to get an audience, soon went back. The naturalist Bonpland, carrying on researches into maté-planting too near to Paraguayan territory to suit Francia, was arrested on Argentine ground and kept prisoner for ten years.

It is futile to deny that Francia conferred some benefits

on his country. In 1819 there was a terrible visitation of locusts, and the crops were destroyed. Francia called the farmers together, and commanded them to sow the land again. Such was the fear of starvation, and the keener fear of being sent to Tevego, the Paraguayan concentration camp in the deserts, or of the " three ball-cartridges " which still oftener followed recalcitrance, that the farmers did as they were told, and found to their amazement that the soil would bear twice in the year.

As for idlers or shirkers, he had his own way with them. The monks were turned out of their cloisters, and driven into the fields or the workshops. A cobbler brought him two belts, which did not satisfy the Dictator. " Take this wretch," said he to a sentinel, " and walk him half a dozen times under the gibbet ; and tell him he shall be hanged with his own belts if he hasn't a decent pair of belts ready for me next morning." It is small wonder that, during the twenty years of Francia's rule, the very character of the people seemed changed. Men worked, in that tropical country, where *dolce far niente* had been specially sweet, as if it had been Lancashire.

This stern vigour Francia maintained, and the fear of him lasted unabated, till he was more than eighty years old. He died on September 20, 1840, and a month later the Rev. Manuel Perez delivered a funeral oration in the Church of the Incarnation at Asuncion, on the text, " When the children of Israel cried unto the Lord, the Lord raised up a saviour which saved them." As given by Carlyle, the sermon is remarkable.

" What measures did not his Excellency devise to preserve peace in the Republic at home and command respect abroad ! His first care was to obtain supplies of arms and to discipline soldiers. To all who imported arms he gave permission to export what produce they wished.

"Whenever a robber was seized, he was led to the nearest guard-house, a summary trial took place, and straightway he was shot. This proved effectual. Ere long, we may say, a child might have travelled from the Uruguay to the Parana without any other protection than the dread of the Supremo.

"When anarchy threatened, it behoved his Excellency to be prompt. He seized the leaders; they were summarily tried, and convicted of high treason. What a struggle now for his Excellency between the law of duty and the voice of feeling! I am confident that had imprisonment seemed sufficient, his Excellency would never have ordered the execution of these men. But God himself approved the conduct of Solomon in putting Joab and Adonijah to death. . . . Dwellers in cities, rest tranquil in your homes; you are a portion of the people whom the Lord confided to the care of our Dictator; you are safe."

There have been, and are, admirers of Francia. But, giving him all the credit possible for the "order" he so ruthlessly secured, we cannot fail to see that it was attended by the inevitable evils. He had so utterly crushed out independence and initiative that when he died there was not a man capable of carrying on his work. He had allowed not even secretaries to exist: there were only machine-made clerks. No one for twenty years had dared to form a decision of his own. Such men of determination as there were had, not unnaturally, thought it safer to hide their talents in obscurity; for Francia, who had read Rollin's *Ancient History*, knew the story of Tarquin and his method of dealing with conspicuous poppies. Thus for some time after his death there was a state of chaos; and it was singularly fortunate for Paraguay that among the men who had survived the tyranny was one of education and intelligence. Carlos Antonio Lopez had been trained in theology at the University of Asuncion, as well as in law and jurisprudence, before the reign of Francia began. He then practised as a barrister, and gained considerable repute in his profession. But Francia frowned on barristers; they might hold and propagate ideas of their own. Lopez therefore retired to his estates, and confined himself entirely to agriculture and to the study of the few books which he had been able to procure—all of which were old. Of events outside the country he could know nothing; for newspapers were stopped on the frontiers. In these circumstances it is astonishing that he was able to acquire such sound ideas: it may be that, looking at the state of the country, he arrived at the view that one was most likely to be right in doing always the opposite of what Francia did.

After months of uncertainty and embarrassment, Carlos emerged into notice, and his talents seem to have been at once recognised. A military head of the State, Don Mariano Alonso, was appointed, with Lopez as his secretary. A few weeks later, the right step was taken: the civil officer was made First Consul and the soldier second. Not a word of censure was uttered as to Francia's acts, but the shootings ceased, six hundred prisoners were drawn out of the dungeons, and some attempt was made to restore the confiscated property to the families which had been ruined by the enormous fines imposed by the dead Dictator. A sigh of relief might have been heard in the country, which had been less grateful for the benefits of the tyranny than readers of Carlyle might suppose. It seemed to prefer the man raised up by itself to the saviour raised up by the Lord. Not the least satisfactory of the changes was the removal of restrictions on external trade. Within three years Lopez became, in perfectly constitutional fashion, President of the Republic; and he signalised his appointment by admitting foreigners freely.

Carlos had his difficulties. Rosas, the Dictator of Argentina—a man not unworthy of comparison with the most determined tyrant that ever lived—had conceived the idea that Paraguay should form a part of the Argentine republic. With this in view, he began by closing the river to Paraguayan trade, and thus checking the incipient commerce of the country. Lopez therefore made an alliance with Brazil and declared war on Rosas; with the result that various complications ensued in which the United States, Britain, and France bore a part. But in 1852 Rosas was deposed, and after the manner of so many South American tyrants took refuge, with a well-filled chest, in England. Peace was made, embassies from foreign countries arrived in Asuncion, traders entered the country, merchant ships plied up and down the river, a period of tranquillity and prosperity set in, and—a matter of considerable importance in the near future—Carlos's eldest son, Don Francisco Solano Lopez, was sent on a mission to Paris and other capitals in order to interest Europe in the possibilities of further trade with Paraguay.

It is said that Don Carlos was regarded with awe or even fear by his ministers; but this was not due to terrorism. He was, in 1857, elected, apparently by free choice, head of the State for ten years—that is, practically for life—and it was understood that he would name his son as his successor. He contrived, also, to reduce the power of the deputies in Congress to a few formalities. With such authority it was not unnatural that he usually succeeded in obtaining prompt obedience; and this was further secured by his command of a strong and ever-growing army, for which the rapidly-increasing wealth and population of the country made it comparatively easy to pay. His military position in South America may be compared with that of Frederick William of Prussia in 1740: his country was in area one of the smallest, but his striking force the most formidable, among all the States in the midst of which he was placed. It remained to be seen whether his successor would allow that force to rust, or whether, like Frederick the Great, he would use it for aggression on his less well-armed neighbours.

The question was soon answered. Don Carlos died in 1862; and his eldest son Francisco Solano succeeded him. Francisco was a most remarkable man. His father had given him a good education, and his diplomatic experiences in Europe had enlarged his mind. He had a thorough knowldge of French, and could thus speak to foreign visitors without needing an interpreter. His quickness and intelligence, as well as his apparent character had won the admiration of those who had met him both in London and in Paris; and many had expressed the opinion that Paraguay was fortunate in having one who would carry on, and improve, the work so well begun by Don Carlos.

But his sojourn in Paris coincided with the second Bonapartist régime, when the "Napoleonic idea" flourished without serious opposition; and Lopez conceived an intense admiration for the great Emperor. He seems, indeed, while yet in Paris, to have formed the determination to play in South America the part which Napoleon had played in Europe: and he certainly studied carefully the means by which Napoleon had won his victories, and which had led the Grand Army in triumph into so many capitals. He was confirmed in these designs by a woman named Madame Lynch, of Irish extraction and French upbringing, whom he met in Paris; and whom, though he never married her, he carried with him to South America and made Empress in all but name. Thenceforward, Madame Lynch was always by his side; and, whatever might be the fate of his other attachments, their mutual affection remained unaltered till the last. There are those who think her his evil genius; it is certain, at any rate, that she never restrained his passions or his violence.

Lopez was thirty-six when his father died. Although he had been named successor, there was some opposition to his election, which he crushed as if he had been the son of Francia rather than the heir of Carlos Lopez. It was not long before people perceived that here was a man who, gracious as his manners might occasionally be, would stick at nothing : and in spite of the material improvements he introduced—he widened the streets of Asuncion and started railways—it was clear that he meant to rule by terror ; and fear rather than gratitude was the dominant feeling in the country. With the Church he dealt more vigorously than Francia himself ; Thompson, the English resident to whom we owe most of our knowledge of his actions, tells us how he reduced the Bishop, Palacio, to the condition of a mere lackey ; the prelate would shuffle to meet his master with a deep bow and a cringing look ; Lopez replied, if at all, with a careless nod. Masterman, a chemist or doctor whom he carried about on his marches, and whom incidentally he imprisoned and tortured, describes him as about five feet four inches tall—the height of his idol Napoleon—with manners charming when he was pleased, but utterly ferocious when he was angry : and his attendants, lay or clerical, were justly careful how they stirred his fury.

His chief attention was devoted to the army, which he continually increased until it reached the portentous strength of eighty thousand men ; and which he disciplined until it bore the same relation to that of neighbouring states as that of Frederick the Great to that of Saxony or Austria. Not unnaturally, these states watched his conduct with anxiety. Apart from other causes of fear, the population of Paraguay, comparatively small as was the area of the country, was greater than that of the huge empire of Brazil, and far greater than that of La Plata or Uruguay : and the country had that central position which added so much to the strength of Napoleon or of Louis XIV.

There would always be an excuse and an opportunity for war. If in 1895 the boundary between British Guiana and Venezuela was uncertain; if in our own day there is dispute about the Chaco, much more uncertain were boundaries seventy years ago, and in districts further removed from rivers or the sea. Much of the territory was still unexplored, and after the expulsion of the Spaniards much had been of necessity left indefinite. In these circumstances quarrels were not uncommon, and the most pacific rulers might be forced to take strong action. Even Don Carlos Lopez had, as we saw, once or twice, gone to war. It was generally held that, in the scramble for land, Brazil had contrived to seize more than her share.

When, therefore, it was observed that Brazil was intriguing in Uruguay on behalf of one of two rival Dictators, she was inevitably suspected of doing so with an eye to her own interest, and Lopez determined to intervene. Could he use the occasion for enlarging his own territory, he would strengthen his position at home; for all nations have shown themselves willing to put up with some loss of liberty if in return they can see their country looking bigger on the map.

The war which followed was one of the most savage and desperate in the whole history of the world. It began in November 1864, and lasted till February 1870: and it is impossible to imagine more utter ruin than the cruelty and obstinacy of Don Francisco brought upon his country. Parallels have often been drawn between the position of Paraguay and that of Germany in the war of 1914: its army was ready, and those of its enemies unprepared; everything depended on a speedy decision. If the potentially stronger nations could hold out at the beginning, their preponderance was almost certain to tell in the end. Nor was this the only likeness which will occur to the reader.

A Brazilian steamer, carrying the Governor of Matto Grosso, was on her way from Rio de Janeiro up the river Paraguay, and necessarily passed Asuncion. Without troubling to declare war, Lopez sent a cruiser to attack her; she was captured and her passengers were brought as prisoners to Asuncion. Brazil was taken by surprise; and for a time could offer very little defence. Several forts on the river were easily seized, and large stores of munitions of war fell into the Dictator's hands. The Brazilian garrisons, assailed by trained and confident troops, had no choice but to abandon the forts, and retreat as best they could. Thus large portions of territory came into Francisco's possession. He now turned his attention from the north to the south. Between him and the Brazilian capital lay the Argentine province of Corrientes—a sort of Belgium. He demanded a free passage for his troops through this province; and on the refusal of the demand declared war on the Argentine. Nor was this all. The Government of Uruguay was hostile to him; accordingly he added Uruguay to the number of his enemies.

At first things went well, and a number of victories were gained on foreign soil. Partly, of course, this was due to the incompetence of armies and commanders not accustomed to regular warfare. Like the North in the American Civil War, they had to learn from defeat: and

Lopez aided them by his own methods. He utterly disregarded losses, and made no attempt to spare either the lives or the health of his men. One of his maxims was that his troops should never, in any circumstances, retreat; and to ensure this he put bands of men in the rear of the fighting line, with orders to shoot any soldier who yielded an inch. As described by Thompson and Koebel, these measures were terribly wasteful and brutally cruel. Every soldier was responsible for the behaviour of five others; every captain for his company, and every higher officer for those below him in rank. Defeat, whether blameworthy or not, was punished with death to the commander and decimation for the army. It may be asked why, in such circumstances, there was not wholesale desertion. All authorities are agreed that the men were eager to desert; but such was the distrust among them, and such the certainty that the first to move would be shot, that there was scarcely a single case of desertion during the whole war. As a further precaution, Lopez adopted the device of holding the wives and children of the officers as hostages; and these, if a failure occurred, were savagely flogged or otherwise tortured.

After two years the tide gradually turned, and Lopez was compelled to substitute imaginary victories for real ones. People were given the strange spectacle of men shot for defeats which the official proclamations represented as triumphs: and indeed so few survived these desperate conflicts that falsehoods were not easy to expose. Every battle became an affair of extermination; for the armies, however hopeless their position, never surrendered.

Every day Lopez became more gloomy and more suspicious. A triple guard surrounded him; his own relatives he ceased to trust and shot for " treason ". A sergeant, entering into trivial talk with Thompson, was shot for " conspiracy ", and his men were punished for looking on.

Little by little the Paraguayan troops were driven back into their own country, or rather, slaughtered outside it; and Lopez had to face invasion. Nothing could have saved him but the amazing sluggishness of the enemy. General Caxias, the Brazilian commander, knew neither the art of winning a victory nor that of following it up when won; nor was Mitre, the Argentine general, much better. On one occasion these strategists allowed an army of twenty thousand to be repulsed by two thousand.

None the less, the end was inevitable. The Allies proclaimed that they had no quarrel with the people of Paraguay—their only enemy was the President who was ruining his own country. With painful slowness they drove his ever-diminishing forces further and further to the north. Asuncion was taken. Starvation drew nearer and nearer, despite the labours of women who were compelled to till and reap the fields—many of them dying from sheer hunger and exhaustion in the work.

The description given of the final scenes is beyond words horrible. The war had degenerated into a chase, delayed only by the necessity of capturing isolated fortresses. In almost every case the garrisons resisted to the death, refused quarter, and were massacred to the last man. Lopez, who usually watched the battles from the rear, constantly eluded the pursuit, burning villages and towns to prevent his enemies from gaining supplies. The resulting misery was fearful. One town, Angostura, actually did capitulate; we hear of no other. Thenceforward nothing was left to the insensate President but a miserable series of flights. At Cerro Leon, far in a wooded and marshy country, he was met by the faithful Madame Lynch, a few officers, and some hundreds of tattered and starving soldiers. The Brazilians advanced on Cerro Leon. Lopez thereupon crossed the Cordilleras, leaving Colonel Caballero perhaps the best of his surviving officers to defend the position of Azcurra. Once more the relentless foe pursued; the Brazilians, under the Comte d'Eu, who, none too soon, had superseded Caxias, came up to the place, and surrounded it on all sides. Caballero was summoned to surrender; but, with the strange stubbornness shown by the Paraguayans throughout this terrible war, refused all terms. He had but fifteen hundred wretches under his command, many of them boys from twelve to fifteen years of age, and the Brazilians had ten thousand soldiers; but he fought to the last. The battle, or rather the massacre, was fearful; women and children perished with the armed men; no quarter was asked or given; and the Paraguayans were annihilated. Caballero was taken alive, and killed in cold blood. This frightful slaughter took place on August 12, 1869.

But Lopez still lived; and while he was alive the object of the war was yet unattained. He might keep up for years a guerrilla struggle like that in which Jugurtha almost wore out the patience of Rome herself. As soon as he heard of the disaster, he celebrated a *Te Deum* for one more pretended victory, and then ordered yet another retreat. His few remaining guns were harnessed to teams of miserable women, and dragged wearily through the swamps and over the passes. A remnant of soldiers still followed him; and he was able for some months more to elude the search of the Brazilian horsemen, and to maintain himself in the almost inaccessible mountains. Burning hamlets marked his path, which might be traced also by the corpses of beasts of burden which were slaughtered as they became useless. Women, when they sank beneath their loads, were left to starve, or, if a fit of mercy took him, were shot by the roadside.

At last, in February 1870, news reached the Brazilian forces that he was on the banks of the Aquidaban, a tributary of the Paraguay. His position would be a few leagues to the north of Concepcion, and two hundred miles north of Asuncion. It might be possible to surprise him; the attempt was made and succeeded. He was discovered, and was found to have still a thousand men and seventeen guns. But the exhausted band made no resistance: in utter indifference they stood or lay, as they were, to be cut down by the advance guard of their enemies. The Brazilian losses were five men wounded. Lopez fled, but was pursued and overtaken. Summoned to surrender, he refused, and was thereupon slain. The six years' war was at last over.

Few worse architects of ruin have ever existed than Francisco Lopez. We think of Genghis Khan and Hyder Ali; but these devastated foreign countries; Lopez wasted his own. It is calculated that in 1864 the population of Paraguay was about nine hundred thousand;

in 1870 there were scarcely three hundred thousand left, and of these less than thirty thousand were grown men. More than thirty-five thousand had fallen, mercifully, in battle; the rest had perished more cruelly by pestilence, starvation, or exhaustion. The country was a desert, the people prostrated, hopeless, broken. For six years a Brazilian army occupied the land, and crushed it, if possible, more than it was crushed already. But for the rivalry between Brazil and the Argentine, indeed, Paraguay would have ceased to exist as an independent state. Sixty years have passed, and new generations have arisen; Nature, more profuse in that tropical region than elsewhere, has covered the battlefields with her kindly mantle of oblivion; but it will be long before men forget the destruction wrought by the evil passions of this man in one of the fairest quarters of the world. Not merely was the land made a solitude; the men that survived had forgotten how to rule it, and for long the fears and suspicions which Lopez had fostered made Paraguay the home of anarchy and discord.

The moral of this terrible story lies on the surface. Assume, for the sake of argument, that you can find a dictator whose rule is on the whole beneficial, and suited to the particular conditions of the state in which he rises. It is not, in fact, easy to find, among the thousand Dictators of history, one more reputable than Don Carlos Antonio Lopez. But how are you to guarantee that his successor will be like him? The good ruler has trained his subjects to a willing obedience, and accustomed them to a not altogether ignoble slavery. How are you to be sure that his son, born in the purple, will not use this tradition of subservience for his own ends, which may be very far from consistent with the happiness of his country?

Again, what if the Dictator goes mad? There is nothing that tends more certainly to dementia than uncontrolled power: and there is scarcely an example in history of a tyrant who has been able to resist the subtle disintegrating forces of success, flattery, the obvious awe and fear of his subjects, and all the other debasing influences of his position, and remain the man he was. You may choose a Bonaparte to be your First Consul; ere long he becomes the Emperor Napoleon, with a besotted belief in his star, and a daily increasing impatience of advice or opposition. Even Julius Cæsar, with all the self-knowledge and simplicity of his character, shows traces of this weakness: he could overcome his enemies, but he could not prevail against the consequences of overcoming them. The calm and clear-sighted man degenerates into the hasty and haughty god. Much more terrible is the case of men who are not Napoleons or Cæsars, and who have not had the advantage, which those great men enjoyed, of having spent years of inferiority or equality to others, in which they had often to meet opposition or contradiction. In men of lesser breed arrogance passes, by insensible degrees, into maniacal frenzy, total inability to grasp actualities, and the madness of cruelty. Francisco Lopez is only the most conspicuous type of such men; the disease, in more or less dangerous form, exists in every man whom fortune sets above his fellows. Unfortunately, it is not easy to put an autocrat into a strait waistcoat. His homicidal lunacy does not, as a rule, become obvious to everybody until it is too late to control it. Even Caligula might have gone on for years in his insanity if he had not become dangerous to his personal guards; and Cambyses fortunately died by accident. Others, unfortunately, have lived on.

Mental disease, of course, may overtake constitutional rulers; but in their case there is no need for their subjects to choose between national ruin and assassination. An Emperor Paul must be put violently out of the way, or Russia will be destroyed. But a George III has ministers who can appoint a Regency; and even a Christian of Denmark, amazing and ridiculous as his behaviour may be, can be restrained. Where, on the other hand, can restraint be found for the man whose followers have deliberately set him above restraint, whom there is no constitution or tradition to control, and who has never learned to put the least check upon his passions?

The story is well-known of the flattering lady who told Alexander I of Russia that if all autocrats were like him there would be no desire for democracy in the world. Alexander replied, " Even if I were what you think me, I should be but a happy accident." History bore him out: he succeeded a Paul and was succeeded by a Nicholas; nay, he himself, within a few years, ceased to be the benevolent despot of Madame de Stael's eulogy. Much more unfavourable is the judgment of history on those who, unlike Alexander, have come to the throne not by legal right, but by violence and fraud.

MODERN TYRANNIES

> "No one man is capable of governing millions."—
> *Henry Marten to Clarendon.*

THE main difference between recently established tyrannies and those we have been considering is that the modern, as a rule, are based on a theory, and are meant to give it political expression. There are of course differences due to the advance of mechanical science; the material means employed to gain power are as unlike the old as the aeroplane and the tank are unlike the pilum or the arrow: and the methods of propaganda are more efficient than those available to a Dionysius or a Peisistratus. The mere physical size of the countries affected is so vastly greater to-day that essential similarities may be disguised. But these are comparatively unimportant distinctions: whereas the other is profound and vital. There is no sign that Phalaris began his assault on the oligarchy of Agrigentum with a philosophical lecture on the relative merits of the system of government he wished to overthrow and of that he desired to establish; and when Abimelech asked the Shechemites whether they preferred the rule of one to the rule of seventy, this was but an *argumentum ad homines*, not a dissertation on politics. But Lenin, Mussolini, and Hitler, each in his special way, had a theory which had been formed, and proclaimed, beforehand, and which, after they had attained power, they proceeded to translate into action. Though this theory might be modified in detail as circumstances dictated, those who supported these aspirants to power knew *what* they were supporting, and not merely *whom*: they had, in a word, an ideal. So far, these tyrannies stand on a somewhat higher plane than those of Dr. Francia, Lopez, or the Greeks. They are not utterly selfish or unpatriotic, nor can we call them definitely hostile to humanity. As Napoleon III, long before he came to the throne, had enunciated the Napoleonic Idea and posed not as a candidate for despotism but as the embodiment of the imperial dogma, so Lenin was not Lenin but Communism, Hitler is National Socialism, Mussolini Fascism. The first Napoleon said, truly, that he was not a man but an Event. These men might say that they are not men but Principles. The State, says one of the most remarkable of them all, Oliveira Salazar of Portugal,* "is a doctrine in action"; and one of his admirers, Paul Valéry, defines a Dictatorship as "the inevitable response of the mind to the demand for authority, continuity, and unity in the nation"; and this idea, he says, always arises in those who wish to

---

* Salazar is indeed a remarkable man. "Our system," says he, "is *like* Fascism, but is adapted to Portuguese mildness. Mussolini is an Italian, a condottiere of the Middle Ages, an over-rigid moralist. Violence like his does not suit Portuguese gentleness. Not that it is not legitimate to defend ourselves with energy when our kindness is abused. It is true that we send our political opponents to islands; but, as Pilsudski remarked: 'Happy Portugal, whose Siberia is Madeira!'

"There are some prisoners who, for political purposes, tell falsehoods as to their treatment in prison. To them we pay no heed. If they tell the truth we relieve them.

"As Christina of Sweden put it, in a note to Machiavelli's *Prince*, we must *now and then* trust others. Much oftener must we pretend to trust them!"

The philosophy of Salazar, which comes to this, that no one must oppose him by word or deed, is beautifully wrapped up in these expressions.

remake society *selon un plan théorique*. It is true than in every case they have had to personify these principles, and to insist on loyalty to themselves as the representatives of the sacred ideas. Salazar, for example, demanded the abolition of all parties in Portugal except the one which agreed with him, which he indignantly refuses to call a party : and Mussolini has done the same in Italy. Such a system it is not unfair to call a tyranny. Like other tyrants these rulers have had to suppress opponents by the most ruthless violence ; but they would say, and probably believe, that they are crushing not rebels but heretics. From a certain point of view one can admire them, as one can admire the fanatical adherents of a religion. There is no reason to think that when they organise massacres or pogroms, crowd the prisons, dot the country with concentration camps, or populate islands with their political opponents, they are as a rule actuated by blood-lust or personal hatreds. They are crusaders crushing the Paynims, or Mohammedan devotees giving the infidel the choice between the Koran and the sword. Their cry is, " The State is one, and Mussolini or Hitler is its prophet."

Various as their ideas are, they are all alike in one point. They all repudiate what, in other countries, is known as individual freedom. " It is not possible," admits, or rather boasts, Salazar, " to erect upon a system of personal liberty any system of guaranteeing effective *legitimate* liberties ; for personal liberty means oppression and every kind of despotism. In its place we put patriotism, the desire for service, the will to obey, discipline, order." No man is to possess his own body or his own soul ; he is to be the slave of the State, to do what the State requires and to think as the State directs. He may fancy he is saving the State; but the State is the sole judge of its own safety, and cannot permit itself to be embarrassed by would-be saviours. To this end the citizen is adopted from birth, surrounded with the desirable influences, given the proper air to breathe, debarred from hearing or seeing anything that might dilute his loyalty, nursed, guided, regulated, moulded into the shape the State deems fitting, and turned into a cog in the State machine. Everything which, in free countries, is held dearer than life, is anathema. So effective is the system that at last the citizen ceases, if he has ever felt his slavery, to harbour even the fleeting suspicion that he is in bonds.

As Goebbels has announced, " The freedom of Germans consists in accepting the higher moral laws of the State willingly and with a sense of responsibility "; and, in thousands of cases this " free " servitude has been accepted as uncompromisingly as a similar servitude is accepted by the saints who have overcome their own desires and become the bondsmen of Christ. The State is " totalitarian "; that is, it is all in all. Art for the sake of art exists no longer; religion is a Government department; education has to be devoted to the glorification of the régime, and excludes everything that can possibly tend to its disparagement; the newspapers and the wireless tell no more and no less than they are allowed to tell; and the least whisper of dissent is carried, by birds of the air, from the bedchamber to the ears of authority.

As one manifestation of this hatred of democracy, it goes without saying that none of these " Dictatorships " will tolerate real Parliaments, and many of them have discarded even such phantom Senates as the Roman Emperors permitted to propose measures suggested from above, and to vote in accordance with the Imperial will. Debate assumes that a proposal has imperfections; interpellations mean criticism; and arguments imply a doubt of the infallibility of the secular Pope. It is noteworthy that many of the Dictators have been in their time members of Parliament, and have been disgusted with Parliamentary " futility ": that is, they have often found that their plans have failed to gain the assembly's approval. Such failure is annoying to anybody, and most of all to a man of autocratic disposition. So soon as he gains power, therefore, he puts Parliaments in their place. He may permit trade-councils, Soviet-assemblies, and other subordinate bodies; but he will have nothing which may dispute the power with himself. Even so mild a ruler as Cromwell felt this impossibility. He would convene Parliaments; but when they began to discuss his right even to convene them, he dissolved them. As for Napoleon, he became restive when Talleyrand told him he had founded nothing permanent until he had set up institutions strong enough to oppose him on equal terms. Much more decisively does the modern Dictator refuse to acknowledge the possibility that any organisations may represent the popular will better than he does himself. *L'État, c'est moi* is his creed, and he defends it by very drastic anathemas.*

---

* To compare great things with small, I may illustrate this from Coleridge's anecdote about the Christ's Hospital of his time. " Boy ! " I remember Bowyer (the Head Master, of flogging celebrity) saying to me once when I was crying the first day of my return after the

Not that the State need, at all times and in all circumstances, obey *itself*. It may issue a Constitution, or a Charter of National Unity, but to bind itself to abide by it would be to submit to abstractions, and to diminish its practical powers, which are absolutely unlimited. Thus many of these totalitarian States have found it advisable to modify the principle of equality in favour of the army, which is a convenient instrument for the suppression of malcontents, and is therefore allowed privileges denied to those classes which are not in a position to insist upon favours. In certain cases the Church has been able to make terms; in others, where it might prove a dangerous opposing force, as in Russia and Germany, it has been either crushed or emasculated. But Trades Unions, combinations of workers, and above all, Liberal or Socialistic organisations, have been put down with remorseless energy. At any moment, in fact, the State may remould the constitution on which it is founded, tear up its charter of incorporation, or break the promises which, in its early struggles, it made to gain help. It is its own law, and can break the law.

But while the modern despotisms differ in this marked respect from the ancient, their methods, and the circumstances in which they find their opportunity for forcing themselves on the country are the same; and their tendencies, when once they are established, show a close resemblance to those we have had occasion to notice.

---

holidays—" Boy! the school is your father. Boy! the school is your mother. Boy! the school is your brother, the school is your sister, your first cousin, your second cousin, and all the rest of your relations! Let's have no more crying."

The Hitlers and Mussolinis are Bowyers of a larger growth.

It is all but inevitable that the character of the despot himself should degenerate as time goes on. Even in Julius Cæsar we have traced an impatience of contradiction, a belief in fatalism, and overweening pride, intensifying with success, and feeding on flattery: and in lesser men the process is clearly visible to-day.

All the modern systems, like all the ancient, took their beginning in a real or invented national emergency. In Greece, Metaxas seized power, and induced the King to break his promises, by discovering a Communist danger which nobody else had suspected to exist.* In Portugal, Salazar, who preferred to remain in the background while General Carmona took the popular eye as the nominal President, emerged from his retirement in Coimbra University only when the finances of the State were in confusion, and then, like a monetary prestidigitator, amused the public with dexterously-balanced budgets.† In Italy,

* Metaxas is interesting as perhaps an exception to the rule that modern dictators have a theory. No one has heard from him a single sentence conveying a positive idea. "The emergency came so suddenly," said he, "that I had no time to think of any plan." But even he has got as far as the announcement that "the disciplined attachment to a single purpose, the rhythmical repetition at regular intervals of the same thought, the same sentence, the same movements, have an hypnotic effect"; and on this he will base his system of government. Meanwhile the isles of Greece are being crowded with men who dislike these rhythmical repetitions; and the editors are being told they are mere captains under the general, to pass on his orders to a people of common soldiers.

Metaxas, who started his revolution on August 4, 1936, is the latest, but perhaps not the last of the men to whom other people's thoughts are troublesome, and who therefore send the thinkers to prison.

† Salazar's ideas are given in a series of interviews with a journalist, Antonio Ferro, which have been translated into French by de Castro. These show a remarkable power of wrapping up very concrete actions in abstract expressions. What they really mean is shown by the herds of prisoners crowded in Madeira, and by a letter in *The Times* of October 29, 1936, from a number of distinguished Portuguese exiles, who say significantly that, living as they do live, away from their

Mussolini had a real crisis to deal with, but his journalistic and other propaganda grossly exaggerated its seriousness, and of set purpose hindered the Government in its task of meeting it : he troubled already disturbed waters in order to fish in them.

In the case of Russia the ground was prepared during scores of years by a weak, corrupt, and cruel despotism. only those who saw the working of that despotism can realise how grinding it was, and how ruinous to the country it misgoverned. In its own interest it deliberately encouraged the ignorance of the masses, and, in alliance with a Church nearly as corrupt as itself, cultivated a degrading superstition, and persecuted all forms of intelligent religion. Spies were everywhere, and often "double-crossed" their employers. The Czar was a figure-head, dull, feeble, and narrow-minded. For the reformer, however moderate, there was Siberia. The reply of the revolutionaries was assassination, which bred fear, and the fear bred insane terrorism. Among the twenty per cent. of the population who could read, there was—with the exception of those in Government posts—but a single mind, and that one of either determined or resigned antagonism. It did not need a prophet to foresee that this house of cards could not last. Sooner, rather than later, it must collapse.

Like all such despotisms, this government had no method of dealing with discontent but force, and by force it added to its enemies. The Czar had become, in 1809, Grand Duke of Finland, and as such had bound himself

native country, in England, *they can say what they think*. Behind Salazar's grand phrases there is the most ruthless cruelty and savage repression.

to maintain the constitution of that country, of which he was no more the Czar than George III was King of Hanover or Elector of Great Britain. But this oasis in the midst of absolute monarchy did not suit the bureaucracy which really ruled; and in 1899 Finland was incorporated in the Czardom—an act condemned as illegal by every international lawyer in the world. The result was a system of passive resistance, the growth of Social Democracy in the country, assassination, and the addition to the Empire of three millions more potential revolutionaries. Stupidity, even military stupidity, could go no further.

In 1904 the war with Japan broke out, and a revelation of Czarist incompetence was made to the world, quite appalling in its suddenness. Even with all this incompetence, Russia would have won the war but for the sense that it was utterly unpopular, and that the discontent might at any moment break out into revolution, in which the army might take part. Though Japan was at the very end of her resources, and another two months would have brought her to her knees, a peace was therefore made, which humiliated even those who had opposed the whole enterprise. Next year the intelligentsia rebelled, and the Czar granted a constitution, which, with the inconsistency of weakness, he soon recalled. Many of the rebels were sent to Siberia, there to await their chance.

In the Great War, incompetence, treachery, and corruption once more defeated the army. It was not Germany, but Russians themselves, that broke Russia down. This time the vengeance was to be complete, and if anything could intensify the shame of it, it was mainly engineered by Jews, whom the Czarist system had persecuted more savagely than perhaps any other section of its subjects. A feeble Liberal rising was strong enough to depose the Czar and to sweep away the bureaucracy; but in a very short time a man who knew his own mind came to sweep away the remnants of Czarism and Liberalism together. Deliberately permitted, by the short-sighted calculations of the German generals, who thus hoped to break the Russian military power, Lenin and a band of other Communists invaded the country, not, like so many other revolutionary leaders, to " save society ", but utterly to destroy it, and to build another society on its ruins. Lenin had studied Karl Marx as fanatical Moslems used to study the Koran, or Calvinists the Pauline Epistles; and he had absorbed with terrifying conviction the doctrine of the class-war. I had almost written " with passionate conviction "; but Lenin had the serenity of the man who has no doubts. Bloodshed was nothing to him; the slaughter of hundreds of thousands, so long as they were bourgeois, never cost him a moment's loss of sleep; the upper and middle classes were to him what the Albigenses were to a Papal Crusader. The result was what is so often seen when a determined and united minority faces a majority divided and irresolute. The Bolsheviks were certainly not more than a few myriads among scores of millions; but they knew what they wanted and how to get it. Lenin began by offering the poor agricultural toilers the lands of their quondam masters; and the vast multitudes of moujiks took their chance; they became landowners, and were resolved to remain so.

There might be some capitalists who remained alive. These Lenin crushed more effectually than by the rifle or the sword; he made the currency—the capitalist "measure of value and medium of exchange"—not worth the paper it was printed on. He was at war; and he was only carrying to its logical conclusion the usual cheat of war-time—that debasement of the coinage which Henry VIII practised in England and which was far more fatal a crime than all the executions which have given him so sinister a name.

But the Bolsheviks were aided also by their enemies. They were missionaries, and their propaganda in foreign countries terrified the capitalist nations to such an extent that they went mad. In their panic folly, forgetting all the lessons of history, they endeavoured to assist the Russian adversaries of Bolshevism against Russians. As Austria and Prussia, in 1792, aided French Royalists against French Republicans, and thus rallied millions of Frenchmen to defend what before had been a mere party, so the foreign abettors of the White armies strengthened the cause they hated. The adventure failed, and deserved to fail.

In other respects the parallel with the French Revolution, which so many people drew, was utterly misleading. That Revolution was, in the first instance, a rising of the middle classes, and aimed at moderate reform. Had those reforms been honestly conceded, had there been no *arrière pensée* in the minds of those who ruled, and had there been no treacherous appeals for foreign aid, the movement might well have stopped with reform, more especially as its leaders were numerous, and were divided among themselves. In Russia, on the contrary, an entire upheaval was the aim from the first, and the guiding spirit was one resolute, immovable, and ruthless man, whose will dominated his followers, and suppressed all dissentients. Lenin was a despot of the kind we sometimes see, resolved to rule himself in order to bring about the rule of the common people, whom he regarded as embodied in himself. "Freedom" was to be gained by tyranny. At what point the tyranny was to be resigned, he did not say, and probably did not know. But its place was never to be taken by what Western nations know as democracy. The people, in fact, were to be liberated when they had fully consented to be slaves. Even before Lenin died this consummation had been largely attained; and now, after twenty years, when a new generation has grown up, observers are struck with the cheerfulness and hopefulness of millions of men and women who are obeying the will of a single man over whom they have no control. Poets and novelists in vast numbers put this happiness into words—and without being ordered to do so. It is an invisible and impalpable compulsion. The child has been trained up in the way he should go, and now that he is old he has no will to depart from it.

Since then, the Bolshevik movement has gone on its course. Lenin found himself compelled, in some degree, to modify his extreme Marxism. Under Trotzky, his successor, the process went a little further; but Trotzky could not renounce the doctrine that Bolshevism must propagate itself, by fair means or foul, throughout the world. Here he found himself in opposition to a man of more practical mind, a Georgian named Stalin, who, in his anxiety to carry out the experiment without hindrance, wished to leave other countries alone, and make Russia rather an example than a menace. Trotzky was banished; and, very recently, his chief supporters were tried for conspiracy against Stalin. Guilty or not, they were convicted and executed. At the moment, Stalin seems stronger than ever. If, as he obviously desires, he can keep peace with his neighbours, his amazing experiments may succeed. If they succeed, their results, throughout the world, may be portentous.

In Italy things were similar amid difference. After the conclusion of the war there was bitter disappointment and disillusion: and for this the Allies were in part to blame. To gain Italian help, the people had been led to expect vast extensions of territory, not merely at the expense of Austria and Hungary, but in Asiatic Turkey; and the populace was obsessed with the common fancy that their individual happiness would be increased by the increase in the area of the State. The Saturnian age was to return; the men would thus be consoled for having fought a war in which the glory gained was in inverse ratio to the suffering, and in which the nation had been humiliated by being rescued from utter disaster only through foreign aid. And even this consolation was largely denied. A small portion of Austria was annexed, and a fragment of Hungary. Smyrna was given—an added mockery—to Greece: and, though Greece speedily lost it, Italy felt no satisfaction. At the Peace conference, Orlando, the Prime Minister, though said to be the most logical of all the delegates, found logic of no use as an instrument of persuasion. His arguments were syllogistically irrefragable, and were politely ignored. President Wilson had been no party to the secret treaties, and had no intention of fulfilling the promises of others, more especially as they ran counter to every principle of his Fourteen Points: and the other allies were only too glad to forget they had ever made the promises. Had they, indeed, wished to fulfil them, they were utterly unable to do so: and Orlando returned home, with peace but without honour. Not unnaturally he fell from such power as he had. It was hardly a compensation for such failure that, if a well-known story is true, all Mediterranean questions were submitted to the Italian delegation, and that therefore one of the greatest men then in Paris, not celebrated for geographical knowledge, told a Danzig mission to put its case before Orlando and his colleagues.

Meanwhile, at home, the confusion which always follows a long war, successful or not, was almost as frightful as in Germany or Austria. Prices were high, and, still worse, were constantly changing; starvation was an ever-present menace; fear and discontent were universal. It must be remembered, also, that the country was not yet really homogeneous; the union brought about by Cavour and Garibaldi was largely factitious; Naples did not sympathise with Piedmont, nor Sicily with Lombardy. Parliamentary government, introduced at a time when the British system was almost universally believed to be a cure for all political ills, had not yet found itself: many of the members were corrupt, and factions were numerous and often unmanageable.

Amid the chaos came the news from Russia, which had stirred even our own troops in France, and which found much more inflammable material in Italy. The Lenin revolution was before the eyes of thousands of despairing and impoverished men, who saw in a similar revolution the only way to the recovery of self-respect or even to continued life. There was an uneasy feeling that Italy was despised abroad; Lenin might be hated, but he was certainly not despised. It may be that Russian emissaries fanned the flame; but they were not needed. Bolshevism was a necessary outgrowth of the prevalent misery, and required no intensive cultivation. The Red Flag was openly flaunted, and Communist slogans were everywhere heard. A curious feature of the time was the unpopularity of the soldiers, who were far from finding their country a land fit for heroes to live in; and they, resenting their unpopularity, added another element to the general unrest. Many of them turned Bolshevik for the very reason that they were hated by the Bolsheviks. A general strike in 1919 was at once a symptom and an aggravation of the feeling in the country. Here was the opportunity of Communism. The Red Guards were still a minority, but in no greater a minority than their Russian brethren had been in 1917. They would almost certainly have seized power if they had known how to use their chances.

The regular Government, at this crisis, was not altogether helpless: but it had great difficulties to contend with. Parliament was divided. Its conduct of the war had not been conspicuously capable; the Church did not trust it, the wealthier classes had little belief in it, and the poor hated it as a bourgeois instrument. Nevertheless, the Government acted with some vigour. The strikes were reduced in number from two thousand to one thousand; and it is likely that if the Prime Minister had been properly supported, order could in time have been restored. For the Bolshevik party had no leader, or—what is the same thing—leaders they had many. Chaos was more chaotic in their ranks than in the country at large, and next to it, " high arbiter, chance governed all ". The danger was less great than it seemed : the old Roman maxim, " Divide et impera ", if applied vigorously against men already divided, might have had its usual effect. From a distance Lenin was watching, and trusting that a man might be thrown up to bring order into the confusion ; but he watched in vain, and so long as no such man arose, the country could be hopeful of escaping disaster.

There was a man who might, from his previous history, have been expected to prove the desired leader. In 1922, Benito Mussolini was just under forty. He was a Socialist, and editor of a journal called significantly *Il Popolo d' Italia*. He had been in prison for his creed. He had served in the war and had been wounded ; he had learned to despise the higher command, and had, not unnaturally, exaggerated the incompetence of the Government. The disaster of Caporetto had deeply impressed him. His creed may be summed up in a phrase of his own, " the aristocracy of the men in the trenches." Thus he had much in common with the Red party ; he was a Leninist in his contempt for Parliaments and for the so-called democratic constitution ; and he was a revolutionary. But he was a Nationalist, and would have nothing to do with a movement which was international or nothing. As his phrase shows, he had little sympathy with the hatred of the soldiery; though he did not dislike disorder in itself, he detested disorder which did not further his own ends : and while he could foster confusion, he did so merely in order at the right time, to appear as the one man who could rule the wild uproar. Thus, to the surprise and disappointment of many in Italy and of Lenin abroad, he drew apart from those who might have been expected to be his natural allies. While the Reds were uncertainly groping hither and thither, he was forming his society, " Fasci di Azione Revoluzionaria", Bundles of Revolutionary Action,* named from the fasces or signs of consular office carried by the Roman lictors; and while the Government was proceeding slowly with its work, he was proclaiming that he preferred fifty thousand rifles to five million votes. Both Government and Bolsheviks were loose and divided; his fasces were bound together; and if a threefold cord is not quickly broken, much longer time is needed to break a bundle of a score of rods.

The opening day of his mission may be said to have been March 23, 1919. On that day, in a palazzo at Milan, which was the centre of his journalistic activity, he addressed his followers, and announced his principles of action : which, at that time, were scarcely more than negative; they were anti-Bolshevik and anti-anarchic and little besides. He stood, like Louis Napoleon in 1848, as the representative of order. At first he seemed

* The word was not invented by Mussolini; it had been in use in Sicily for some time.

to have little chance ; but his cause was greatly strengthened by the folly of his adversaries, who not only allowed innumerable outrages, but forgot Danton's wise maxim, that neither killing nor dying, in revolutionary times, should be indulged in without a "useful" purpose. They killed indiscriminately. They ran counter, also, to patriotic feeling, and made no attempt to conciliate the old soldiers. Openly proclaiming Republican doctrines —of their own peculiar brand—they set the Royalists against them ; and, though the royalist feeling was not of the old English Cavalier type—to many the dynasty was still foreign—it counted for something. What was still more important, such capital as was left in the country after the war, the strikes, and the massacres, was, if not for Fascism, against Bolshevism. Mussolini was further aware that there were in Italy, as there are in all countries, multitudes of people who hold the opinion expressed by old Phaonius to the tyrannicide Brutus, that civil war is worse than tyranny, and martial law better than no law at all. He therefore, though not in the least more scrupulous about murder than his enemies, murdered with discrimination, and discouraged outrages that had no point. Though, at first he met massacre with massacre and robbery with robbery, he recognised that reprisals usually defeat their own end, and called loudly for a halt. To a great extent he was obeyed ; and such murders as still went on, though he found it desirable to wink at them, grew fewer, and became more and more "useful" in their character. They were systematic and successful ; and Mussolini was content with disowning them ; he did not punish the perpetrators. At last they were no longer necessary; for the Fascists, by always attacking the opposing leaders, such as the Socialist mayors of towns, or the chiefs of Co-operative stores, terrorised them into resignation; and the Labour Unions came over to Fascism in shoals to save their hard-won property. The effect of this was twofold. As always happens when alliances are formed, one ally influenced the other. Inevitably, Fascism became considerably more Socialistic than it had been, while the power of the landowners, financiers, and business men, whether within the Fascist organisation or approving of it from without, suffered a distinct diminution, though they did not actively oppose the movement. On the other hand, the loss of so many former adherents impelled such Bolshevik leaders as remained to make a desperate effort to recover their position. In July, 1922, a general strike was proclaimed. This was a fatal mistake; for it enabled Mussolini, who had so far failed to gain any countenance from the nominal Government, to plead necessity as an excuse for direct action. It has since been asserted by the Liberals either that he himself engineered the strike or that the danger was slight, and that the Government was quite capable of dealing with it. Whatever the truth may be, he accepted the challenge, ignored the Government altogether, turned his followers into an army of blacklegs, and broke the strike. He could now proclaim that, in the midst of what he designated as an appalling peril, the civil magistrate had failed, and he alone had saved the country. The Communist remnant, now losing all sense of proportion, played again into his hands; in utter recklessness they drove out all their more moderate members, and stood forth at last in open opposition, not merely to Fascism but to the nation itself. They were now not a party, nor even a faction, but rebels, and rebels who, in ordinary times, would have been suppressed without difficulty by the regular government, or even by the ordinary course of law.

But the regular government was at this moment paralysed from within. Facta, the Prime Minister, hesitated in the presence of two enemies. It would appear that, without royal permission, he did not dare to appeal to the Army; and the King was by no means eager to risk a mutiny. Such endeavours as Facta made, without being able to apply force, were thus feeble and futile. Mussolini, after carefully feeling his way, demanded permission, as the Pitt who alone could save the country, to form his own government. Facta offered him a post in the ministry; he contemptuously refused it. He reiterated his demands, this time to the King himself: for though in the past he had been an ardent Republican, he now recognised that Royalist strength was not to be despised, and he proclaimed that the King was to be a real King, free from the shackles of an effete constitution —with mental reservations which became visible later. Certain judicious pronunciamentos further secured the support, or at least the neutrality of the Church. Meanwhile his agents were busily working, especially in the non-industrial South. The ground being thus prepared, he announced from Naples, on October 22, "The South of Italy is ours already. The government of the whole country must be surrendered to us, or we shall march on Rome and take it."

The air all over Italy was tense with expectation. What would Facta do? What would the King do? Would the Reds make another despairing effort? Mussolini was waiting at Milan, and the people were waiting everywhere else. Some were full of hope; others were indignant at the insolent claim; many were afraid; many more, in fatalistic apathy, were ready to accept the result whatever it might be. Even now, perhaps, had the Government moved first, it might have won. But it remained passive; and, after five days, a message reached Mussolini, "It has begun". With the loss of a dozen lives, the Blackshirts had captured the public offices at Cremona. The news was followed by the publication of multitudes of manifestos. The threatened march on Rome might start at any minute.

But Mussolini knew well that the threat of force is often more potent than its actual exercise. He drew his hovering legions round Rome, but did not advance upon her: and with every hour of delay the fear grew tenser. Facta made one more attempt to induce the King to appeal to the regular army; the King again declined. No one can say whether the army would have obeyed him; there are some who believe that the King, by lifting his little finger, could have crushed the infant Hercules in its cradle. What is certain is that the finger was not lifted.

The Blackshirts drew slowly nearer. Mussolini, from Milan, refused to discuss the smallest point; his demand was absolute and unconditional—"I must form my own Government". At noon on the 29th the King agreed by telephone; Mussolini asked for confirmation by telegraph, the confirmation came in a few minutes. He was now

Prime Minister. He formed his cabinet, bade his forces advance, and next day made his triumphal entry, like a victorious pro-consul of old, into the city—except that a pro-consul was not permitted to triumph for a victory over his own people. The constitution had fallen, through the causes enumerated by Dr. Johnson in *Irene*:

> "A feeble Government, eluded laws,
> A factious populace, luxurious nobles,
> And all the maladies of sinking states."

He turned his forces into a volunteer army, enlisted a hundred thousand boy scouts as a nucleus of future armies, gathered round him military men like de Bono and Badoglio, retained a phantom Crown, and issued proclamations to the effect that, as men were tired of liberty, such liberty as was enjoyed in democratic countries should never hold up its head in Italy again. There should be freedom to obey the orders of the State; and " State ", as it soon appeared, was a noun used instead of the first personal pronoun. No opposition was to be permitted; the March on Rome had settled the question as to the right of one party, and one party alone, to dictate opinion.

For the next few months these views were enforced by vigorous arguments. Murder raised its head once more. Bands of Fascists scoured the country, beating opponents, or men who might become opponents, to insensibility or death, or dosing them with castor oil that their agonies might be ridiculous. The ruler took no notice; revolutions cannot be made with rose-water. It is a high tribute to the Italian character that even these outrages did not break the spirit of the successors of Mazzini.

There still remained an opposition, weak in numbers but high in character; and even the defection of three ex-Premiers did not destroy it. Many men, foreseeing their fate if they stayed, emigrated: others remained to face death or torture for their cause. Mussolini and his counsellors grew more and more exasperated and perplexed.

After many months of this sort of terrorism, the time seemed to have arrived at which some show of legality ought to be given to the system; nothing is more characteristic of tyrants that their habit of using force to compel a "legalisation" of force. It was determined to appeal to the country in order to receive its sanction for the new régime. For this end, everything was done to show an impartial witness that the real opinion of the country was not desired. The votes of the whole people were to be added together, and the party gaining the largest number of votes, provided they were more than a quarter of the whole, was to receive two thirds of the seats in the Chamber. To get this extraordinary Bill through the existing Parliament, threats, promises, cajolery, and the appearance of armed Fascists in the lobbies, were freely employed. Only the Socialists dared to vote against it.

The election campaign opened early in 1924. Mussolini began by choosing his own candidates, among whom Orlando and Salandra, two former Premiers, prominently figured. Large sums were secured from the great industrial leaders. In his address, Mussolini declared open war on democracy, announced that Fascism ought not to have submitted to the degradation of an election, and that it did so only to show its magnanimity; added that even if defeated he would still remain in power by the aid of his Fascist militia; and proclaimed that Fascism had *already* trodden on the rotting carcass of the goddess of Liberty. Nevertheless he was plainly intensely anxious to secure a majority. His agents were told to gain complete control of the polling-stations, to keep awkward scrutineers away, and to drive back all Opposition representatives. The presiding magistrates were carefully selected partisans, and were given full instructions as to how to manage the voting. If any of them showed signs of honesty, Fascist delegates were to deal appropriately with them. Open voting was made practically compulsory—" it prevents our adversaries from voting against us." If the magistrates insisted on secrecy, various devices were employed for discovering which of the electors had voted wrong. " Beware, Socialist riff-raff," said a Fascist paper: " we have machine-guns, bludgeons, and our indomitable militia." As a rule the Opposition parties were unable even to present their lists of candidates; in many places, where men abstained from voting, Fascists voted repeatedly in their names. The Secretary of the Fascist party, authorised by Mussolini, issued a circular in Lombardy, commanding that political enemies and even dissentient Fascists were to be treated with such violence as to put them hors de combat; and these acts of violence were to be specially frightful in the earliest elections, so that later electors might know what to expect. Forni, a Milan Fascist, whose creed was too mild for Mussolini, was assaulted and savagely beaten by twenty armed ruffians—in accordance with Mussolini's instructions. " Life," the Duce declared, " was to be made impossible for such men." A Socialist candidate was murdered, and his body was buried without any rites. No one was punished for the crime. An editor who had hitherto supported Fascism, but was neutral in the election, was told by Mussolini that, " his back would be broken."

Even so, the Fascists only received four and a half million votes to two and a half millions ; and in Milan they were actually in the minority. It is strange that Mussolini should have taken so much trouble, and shed so much blood, to gain a victory which everybody could see was in reality a defeat.

A few mock trials for violence and damage followed the mock election. They were entrusted to General de Bono—afterwards not unheard of in Abyssinia—who carefully tried a number of innocent people, acquitted them with perfect justice, and smilingly let the guilty go free.

Of all the murders that of Giacomo Matteotti is the most famous, and—if there can be degrees in such horrors—perhaps the worst. Matteotti was an economist and a Socialist, an Oxford graduate, and a man of extraordinary courage. He had been a member of Parliament for five years, and was, despite the most desperate efforts of his opponents, elected in 1924. He had great skill in the unearthing of facts, and journalistic ability in making them known. After the election, he wrote a book called *Fascism Exposed*, and visited England with a view to having it translated. On his return, he took his seat in Parliament. He knew his life must be short ; but in the time allowed him he meant to do his duty.

The first step of the Government was to propose a law "validating" the election; that is, legalising *ex post facto* whatever had been done to gain the majority. Matteotti rose, and in spite of all interruptions, insults, and threats of murder, delivered a two hours' speech in which the intimidations, corruptions, and falsehoods of the election were exposed. When it was over, he said to a Socialist friend, "You may get ready my funeral oration." Mussolini was furious that he had not been shot in the House itself. Next day a criminal was released from prison, and was told to meet Dumini, a man who had already committed many murders for the great cause. The two scoundrels watched Mateotti's house, waiting their opportunity to take what Mussolini called "concrete action", and what other leaders of the party called "letting the revolver speak." About ten days later, Matteotti, still to his surprise alive, delivered another attack, in Mussolini's own presence, and nonplussing him by quoting from his own words. The *Popolo d' Italia* announced that "coercive measures" were required. One more deed of courage was possible for Matteotti. He put in a Parliamentary question, charging the Government with a long list of crimes, and revealing the brutalities of the local Fascist chiefs. Four days later, Dumini and his fellows seized their victim when he was about to bathe in the Tiber, dragged him into a motor-car, and there shot him dead.

They had been seen, and the number of the car had been taken. Matteotti's papers were handed to Mussolini, and the news of the crime was brought to all the leaders within a few hours. Its echoes reverberated all over

Europe, and the First Murderer was unable to avoid hearing the opinion held of him in every country. He felt no remorse; but he saw the necessity of making excuses. A series of shuffling statements, however, only made matters worse. All knew that his hands were as blood-stained as if they had actually held the pistol. Never were there clearer indications of guilt. Lying statements were made in the Fascist papers: Matteotti had gone to Austria, he had been kidnapped, he had run away from his home. De Bono gave orders to remove the traces of blood from the car—after an interview with the Duce: and in Parliament Mussolini's manner was so halting that he was openly accused of the crime. He sent for Matteotti's widow, and said solemnly, " I would to God I could bring your husband back to life." No sooner had she departed than he said, " There is nothing to be done: there are too many witnesses." He tried to shield himself by throwing over de Bono and others of his associates: but they had already taken the precaution of writing a full account of what they knew, and handing it over to safe keeping. A copy of these revelations was presented to the King, and made it clear to him that Mussolini had personally given orders that Matteotti and other Opposition leaders should be secretly disposed of. It was widely expected that the King would show courage, and dismiss the Fascist ministry: and for some time Mussolini was in visible terror that this might be done. But his Majesty did nothing. Further revelations were made—it was disclosed that the horrible outrages, the murders, the beatings, the administrations of castor-oil, had been done by the leader's express directions. Nothing short of force could silence the cries, which grew louder and louder : and, strong in the royal support, he gave his militia the full armament of the regular troops, arrested hundreds of anti-Fascists, and authorised prefects to prevent the publication of unpleasant truths. In Florence, especially, terrorism was rampant ; houses were sacked, machinery destroyed, shops closed : elsewhere even Church institutions were wrecked. Thus it was sought to prove that the men who were guilty of these villainies could not have been guilty of others. At length the opposition was driven underground ; and the accusing voices were silent. What was no longer talked of might be treated as if it had never happened (as indeed it has been treated by too many in Italy and even elsewhere) and the Duce felt that it was time to call a halt. Open and ostentatious murders and other outrages, which might shock the feebler-minded of his partisans, or rouse indignation abroad, had better cease. But equally horrible cruelties, though less likely to attract attention, were still encouraged and practised : opponents of the régime were not beaten, dosed, or murdered ; they were simply removed from sight. The venue of cruelty was transferred to the dark places of the earth, where it could go on, and still goes on, unnoticed. The world, in its usual fashion, speedily forgot how the tyranny had been founded ; and there were many who, not forgetting, approved of it because it had succeeded. A system of subtle suggestion, and of quiet suppression of everything that could shake the Government, was patiently and persistently practised. Freedom of speech vanished from Italian soil ; and even freedom of thought, which it used to be imagined could never be destroyed, was gradually dissolved away. The press and the wireless were rigidly controlled; and the people were allowed to know only these facts, and thus to form only those opinions, which suited the Duce. Thus has supervened a factitious and meaningless unanimity, always apparent if not quite always real. A sounding phrase was invented to describe the new world. The State was Totalitarian or Corporative. The imaginary happiness of early Rome was restored, when " none was for a party "; for there was only one party to which to belong. All opposition being thus silenced, Mussolini was able, at least in outward show, to follow Machiavelli's advice to the tyrants of four hundred years ago, to get their murders over at the beginning of their reign.

But it was only in outward show. There were the exiles. Some, like Nitti, a former Prime Minister, fled to France, where there is a colony of irreconcilables. The illustrious historian Ferrero has taken up his abode in Switzerland, where a professorship has been given him, and where he has employed himself in writing an account of the greatest of Italian Dictators, Julius Cæsar, in which the history of the past is made a commentary on the present. The hardly less illustrious Professor Salvemini is also an exile; but he has contrived to obtain knowledge of what goes on in Italy and to reveal it, with damning accuracy and astonishing clearness to those—unfortunately too few—who will read his indictment. The distinguished conductor Toscanini, having refused to perform the Fascist Anthem at the Scala in Milan, earned the wrath of the Dictator, and found it desirable to transfer his genius to England. It was like the emigration of the Huguenots from France when the Edict of Nantes was revoked. But for too many emigration was impossible. Thousands of the best men in the country were imprisoned in the islands of the Mediterranean, after mock trials or no trial at all. As in Portugal Salazar has turned Madeira into a Siberia, so Mussolini has made Lampedusa and the Liparis into dungeons. Among the thousands was Nitti's nephew, who had taken no part in politics, but " did not live like other young men "; and it is said that when he escaped his brother was sent to take his place—a device more effective than barbed wire. Among the other thousands was an old Socialist comrade of Mussolini, who had saved the Duce's life in the war, but who had committed the crime of not abandoning his former views.

Since then there is no doubt that the Duce has displayed great ability and skill in his chosen course. In one point, especially, he has acted with a wisdom which it would have been well if some of his imitators had shown. Partly because Italy is in the main of one creed, he has been able, and willing, to make peace with religion. Jews and Protestants are not persecuted as such; and the quarrel between the State and the Church of Rome, which in one form or another had vexed the country for nearly a thousand years, he has settled by a sagacious compromise, not unlike that by which, for a time, Napoleon reconciled State and Church in his Empire. In 1870 the Pope was deprived of his temporary sovereignty, and since that time resided, as an ostentatious self-made prisoner, within the Vatican, never, even during the unhealthy month of August, leaving it for so much as a day. Mussolini has not restored to him the whole realm which, according to the old fable, was given him by the " Donation of Constantine ", and which was confirmed to him by Charles the Great. But he has given him a symbolic substitute. The Pope has received, in full temporal sovereignty, a small region round the Vatican, and is once more, as in the Middle Ages, a king as well as a spiritual pastor. By further concessions as to Catholic education, Mussolini has removed one of the chief difficulties in his way; for a Church which is willing to face martyrdom is, as even Bismarck learned, unconquerable, and is much more desirable as an ally than as an enemy.

Public works of all kinds have simply transformed Italy. The Rome of the Empire has been excavated, and large parts of it have been revealed, after centuries of interment, to modern eyes. Reviving, and carrying to fulfilment, a design of Julius Cæsar, Mussolini has drained marshes. Cities have been cleansed, and sanitation improved out of recognition. Even Naples, according to recent visitors, is now, after fifteen hundred years of filth, a well-scavenged city. The very Italian nature seems to have been transformed: there are no longer the crowds of loungers and beggars which used to meet the eye at every turn; and—*mirabile dictu*—trains run to time and waiters no longer serve by merely standing and waiting. Small wonder that travellers are impressed, and—belonging as they do mainly to the richer classes in their own countries—begin to think that it would be pleasant if something of the kind could be done at home.*

---

* It must be remembered that Liberals are by no means inclined to give sole credit for all this to Fascism. More than a beginning had been made before Mussolini's advent, and he is but continuing the work of others. In fact, just as in the Crimean War Palmerston got

But the price is terribly heavy. The wages of labour, not only nominally but effectively, are incredibly low, and of course no attempt to raise them by strikes or combinations is permitted. The lira, which in 1914 was about 9½d., or one twenty-fifth of the pound sterling, fell to a hundredth by 1918, and under Mussolini it fell again to a hundred and fiftieth; and that though sterling was itself not what it had been. Mussolini in 1927 raised the lira again, by main force, to a ninety-second of the pound, and declared he would defend it to the last drop of his blood. But there are contingencies too strong for the strongest dictators; and in October 1931, though his blood was still circulating, he was compelled to lower the rate by forty per cent. Amid all these fluctuations, there has been no corresponding change in wages. What has further depressed labour has been Mussolini's encouragement of large families—for cannon-fodder is a necessity of imperialism. Though this policy has had far less success than Mussolini expected, yet, so far as it *has* succeeded, it has unfavourably affected labour. The population of Italy is already too great for the resources of a country so poorly adapted by nature for manufactures; and artificially to increase it is only to aggravate misery.

As this fact gradually forced itself even upon minds which have been trained not to think for themselves, a certain discontent became visible, and was too widespread to be ignored or violently suppressed. It was necessary to busy them with foreign quarrels. Hence the Abyssinian

---

the credit for army reforms which had been set in motion by the previous Government, so Mussolini now, say his opponents, is seizing the praise largely due to others.

adventure. It was true that Abyssinia, like Italy, was in the League of Nations, and had indeed been set there mainly by Italian agency. It was true also that Italy had signed a pact with Abyssinia to settle all disputes by arbitration. It was true that an attack on her would be condemned by practically the whole world. But military "glory" was required; and Mussolini cared nothing about promises or treaties; he had plenty of paper on which to write them, and plenty of waste-paper baskets into which to throw them. An excuse was sought, and though not found, was utilised. There had been trouble at Wal-wal, a considerable distance within the Ethiopian border. If anyone was to blame for this, it could obviously not be the Ethiopians; and a League commission absolved them. None the less, Mussolini seized the excuse, and an army of a quarter of a million was gradually assembled in Italian East Africa. One of the most painful features in the whole transaction is the favour shown to it by the Church, the higher dignitaries of which, at least, can hardly have been ignorant of its real character. The Pope himself, who in the early days of the Fascist movement spoke of Mussolini as (like Dr. Francia) a man sent from God, gave his blessing to the enterprise, and lent his Papal troops to the invading army. Cardinals, Archbishops, and Bishops followed suit, and the Papal Secretary of the State praised the "holy conquest". The Virgin herself was declared to be pleased with the victories. Ecclesiastics presented their chains and other ornaments as "gifts to the Fatherland", and the gold and bronze of churches was melted for the expenses of the crusade. A Catholic paper told its readers that Ethiopian troops had attacked Italian native soldiers "at

Wal-wal, in Italian Somaliland ", though a glance at a map would have shown the author of the article the true position of the place. If such was the attitude of religious teachers, one can only be surprised that there was, among the common people, so much opposition to the war as, at the beginning, there actually was.

The result we all know; though the end is not yet. Through the inconceivable folly of the greater League Powers, Mussolini had his way. The one effective sanction—the prohibition of oil—was not put on; Italy was allowed to purchase what it wished, and Ethiopia was allowed nothing. After nine months, in which civilisation showed itself by the ruthless use of yperite on combatants and non-combatants alike, the capital was taken just before the rains set in.

To his own people, Mussolini represented this as a Christianising, cultural, and colonising mission. The Abyssinians were in great part heathen, and in great part Monophysite heretic Christians. They were also barbarians—they had not attained to the use of bombing aeroplanes and poisonous gases. They also had land—and this presented golden opportunities for Italian emigrants. The most glowing pictures were drawn of the possibilities of mining, agriculture, and manufacture. Not a word was said about the climate, the nature of the country, or the general difficulties. It was conveniently forgotten that in Tripoli, which had been annexed in 1912 for similar reasons, and in Libya which was occupied later, colonisation had been a total failure; nor was anything said about the enormous expense of starting the enterprise in Abyssinia even if the conquest should be speedy and complete. The whole thing was a gigantic camouflage; and, as the wireless and the press tell only what they are told to tell, it may be long before the camouflage is seen through. Meanwhile, Italy is plunging as deeply into debt as her inability to raise foreign loans allows her to fall. Once again it is shown that it is not easy to gain wealth by robbery.

In his relations with foreign powers Mussolini has been torn in different directions. He has a natural sympathy with the Naziism of Germany in itself; for, like Fascism, it detests both democracy and Communism. On the other hand, as a Nationalist Italian, he dreads the absorption of Austria by Germany, which is one of the most obvious aims of the Nazis, and which would, if accomplished, bring the most powerful state in Europe into too close a neighbourhood to Italy. Thus, though Dollfuss was a sincere Catholic, and was trying to make Austria a Christian totalitarian State, yet Mussolini assisted him against the Nazis, and the murder of the Austrian Chancellor by Nazi conspirators appears to have deeply moved the Duce. Austria is a buffer State, and must, in Italian opinion, be kept so.

On the other hand, Mussolini is quite willing to work with Hitler in the attempt to weaken Russia, and in the clearly visible purpose to gird the Mediterranean with a ring of Fascist countries. Portugal was already Fascist; Greece was tending that way; Turkey was under the control of one of the most thorough despots in the world. There is a large Fascist party in France. Spain remained; a country which, despite all the efforts of the Hapsburgs and the Bourbons, had never been a unity. Catalonia, in particular, after the most ruthless massacres and punitive expeditions, had scarcely ever ceased to demand Home Rule or even independence; and, since it had been industrialised, the demand had been stronger than ever. After the expulsion of King Alfonso, and the failure of Primo de Rivera's dictatorial rule, Communism, Socialism, Liberalism, and antagonism to the Church, had shown a rapid growth. In the recent election, they had actually gained, though not an absolute majority, a legal Government. Immediately, merely waiting for some act, on the part of the Government, which might form a plausible excuse, Franco, a general in Morocco, Mola, Lliano, and other soldiers, supported by the Church, started a rebellion. They expected, by the suddenness of their attack, to take the Government unawares; in this they failed, and the civil war which followed lasted much longer than they anticipated. As the vast majority of the people were against them, they would now have had no chance without foreign aid: but this was forthcoming in abundance. Fascist Portugal threw open its passes into Spain; and Mussolini and Hitler provided the aeroplanes and the pilots by whose aid thousands of Moorish soldiers were carried across the straits. Munitions of every kind poured in to Franco's assistance, and encouragement of every kind was given to the rebels. Though, from time immemorial, it has been recognised that a government legally constituted may purchase arms from other countries to put down a rebellion, France and England hesitated to use the right. They were afraid of war. They therefore proposed that neither side should be aided: which, in effect, meant favouring the rebels: for, though Germany and Italy agreed " in principle ", in practice the process went on ; and for a long time Portugal did not agree even in principle. The result was at first what might have been expected : the rebels gained ground.

None of these munitions have been paid for in money—Franco has none. What the *quid pro quo* is can as yet only be guessed ; but it is freely said, and as freely denied, that the patriotic general has promised Majorca to Italy. As for the pacific plans, and commissions of inquiry, and gentle remonstrances, of the two democratic nations, Mussolini promises, breaks his promise, and has the debaters in derision. His successful Abyssinian bluff has encouraged him to try another. But such methods involve him in difficulties. To stir up rebellions and troubles all over the world involves the possibility of war, and war means expense. The perpetual threats frighten other nations. As the Mediterranean takes more and more the appearance of an Italian lake, it is not surprising that even sluggish Great Britain becomes anxious ; and a visit of Sir Samuel Hoare to Malta and Cyprus emphasised her anxiety. The Italian answer was a huge extension, at fabulous cost, of munition factories, ship-building, and the construction of aeroplanes. As the State is already practically bankrupt, the resulting misery must be great, and may well lead to discontent which even the most imaginative propaganda will be unable to quell. When Napoleon's finance minister told him that the country was poor and needed peace, " Au contraire," said the Emperor, " il faut la guerre." His idea was to enrich France by robbing other nations. Even in his time the idea was a gross error : to-day it is the wildest of stupidities.

Nations, as has been repeatedly shown, are so closely bound together that even a victorious war is ruinous. That Mussolini does not see this, or, seeing it, ignores it, is sufficient to deprive him of the character which some claim for him, width and greatness of mind.

The case of Germany would take volumes to explain in full. We have here " an old and haughty nation, proud in arms." After the catastrophe of the Thirty Years' War, divided and subdivided into three hundred and sixty principalities, she was the prey of invaders, and lost the very conception of patriotism—a feeling which, said Goethe, " I cannot in the least understand." Napoleon roused the feeling from slumber, and, despite himself, helped to make Germany a nation. The principalities were reduced to thirty-nine; and a sort of federal unity was gained, which was transformed by Bismarck into a Prussian hegemony, based on " blood and iron." In three short and successful wars many of the smaller countries were annexed by Prussia, a complete revenge was taken on France, and the King of Prussia became German Emperor. To the resulting national pride, and the adoration given to soldiers, it is impossible to find a parallel. It is hard to see why millions of people should be proud because some thousands of them have won a few battles; but all victorious nations are illustrations of the strange truth—not least our own people after the Seven Years' War.* There has however been

* It was in the full flood of this national boastfulness that Goldsmith, who as an Irishman was more or less impartial, wrote of the English in the famous lines:

nothing like the German variety of this self-exaltation. Even the Romans admitted the intellectual superiority of the Greeks; but the Germans regarded themselves as the superiors of all other nations in art, science, business ability, and all forms of culture.

The shock to all this when the war ended was terrible, and the more so because a stupid military censorship had kept up the delusion of constant victory to the very end. The crash came with appalling suddenness; and the pride gave way to a sense of utter humiliation. The Allies did nothing to alleviate the feeling. Some Provinces were occupied, others taken away on the ground that they had been unlawfully annexed; and the crowning insult came when the German delegates were forced to accept a dictated peace, and even to sign a declaration, which everybody knew was worthless, that Germany was responsible for the war. Ludicrous indemnities were imposed, which, though all intelligent people knew they could never be paid, were sufficient to plunge the finances into utter confusion.

The Government was Socialist, and did its best in an impossible position; but it was naturally blamed for its failures. A new generation began to grow up, and to ask questions. *Why* was there this universal sense of inferiority? Why should the great German nation, once by common consent the greatest in the world, be so degraded, and accept its degradation? The old spirit must be still there; it only needed to be rekindled. O for

> Pride in their port, defiance in their eye,
> I see the lords of humankind pass by.

The stupidest of Englishmen thought himself a superior being because Wolfe had defeated Montcalm.

a Man ! Let some one arise to lead them, and they would show the world that Germany was what it had been ! They were thus ready to welcome the most obvious falsehoods, if only they were touched with hope. Long before, many falsehoods had been eagerly received. Germany had never really been defeated : her armies had been stabbed in the back : and the Jews had been behind it all, assisting, and assisted by, Bolshevik propaganda, which had stealthily sapped the noble spirit of the people.

Germany was admitted to the League ; but did not yet feel herself treated as an equal. Stresemann asked timidly for some " sample " arms, as a symbol that she was no longer a pariah among the nations : for the German idea that the greatness of a nation is determined by the greatness of her military forces was not dead. Whether Stresemann might ultimately have been the Messiah of the public longing none can tell ; he died before he could be tested. The aged President Hindenburg was *magni nominis umbra*, a shadow and a figurehead. It was doubtful whether he even understood the documents he signed. People were waiting : something was sure to happen.

Adolf Hitler—to use the pseudonym by which he has chosen to be known to the world—was not precisely a German. He was an Austrian, but an Austrian whose desire was that his native country should be absorbed into the larger Teutonic world : and this is not surprising, for he was born at Braunau, almost on the exact dividing line between the two countries. He had seen the direst poverty face to face, and never ceased to regard himself as one of the people. The marked separation of classes prevalent in Germany fretted him : and he became early a passionate believer in equality. He served in the war; and this belief was strengthened by his experiences. But added to it was an even more passionate feeling—that of German nationality, unity, and greatness; and he sought for an explanation of the crash which had so suddenly overtaken the obviously greatest nation in the world. He was peculiarly susceptible to atmosphere, and he absorbed and assimilated, with astonishing speed and force, the ideas floating around him. During the Socialist rule he tried to put some of these ideas into action. Things were not yet ripe; and he was imprisoned after the failure of a "Putsch" in which he took part along with Ludendorff. In prison, where he had light and leisure (the jailors not being Nazis) he set down his ruling notions at portentous length. Some of these were those which had been popularised before the war by Houston Stewart Chamberlain. Germans were Nordics, "Aryans" of the blonde race, which was higher than all others, and to which belonged every great man who had really moved the world, Leonardo, Dante, Shakespeare, and Jesus Christ himself, who, divine or human, was at any rate not a Jew. This fancy, derided by every serious anthropologist in the world, had delighted the Kaiser, and now captured Hitler. That no nation is pure, and that the Germans are perhaps more completely mixed than any other, was a truth which Chamberlain ignored and Hitler frantically denied. As for the Jews, they were the enemies of the human race: and the Communists (who were largely Jews) were no better. It was these who had, first, engineered the war, and then, for their own purposes, brought about defeat. They had craftily stolen all the best positions in the country: they had, in countless numbers, occupied professorial chairs, posts in hospitals, ruling positions in banks; and all these places they used as vantage grounds for destroying the country. They were the lowest and the most cunning of peoples, and yet so stupid that, having climbed to the highest point of the tree, they spent all their energies in sawing away the branch they sat on. They must therefore be crushed—the internal enemy must be made helpless. After that, the foreign nurse of Communism must be destroyed—Russia must be invaded and overthrown, and her most fertile province, the Ukraine, annexed; such annexation was desirable for Germany, and therefore right. When Russia had been thus broken " we could settle with France "—a phrase afterwards skilfully modified, in the English version of the book, into "arranged".

As for Germany herself, all Germans were to belong to her, whether in Austria, or in Czecho-Slovakia, or in fact anywhere; and these Germans, thoroughly purged of "non-Aryan" elements—of everybody, in fact, who had the slightest taint of Jewish blood—must be *one*. The old divisions must be abolished: there must no longer be a Bavaria declaring war a day later than Prussia as a symbol of semi-autonomy, nor an Austria actually independent, nor a free Danzig. Nor must there be class-distinctions— the nation must be Socialist, but National also; self-contained, self-sustaining. Hence the expressive abbreviation *Nazi*. All parties must be abolished—for the Nazis, like the Fascists, were not a party. Religion, too, must be national, or it must go.

As with other portentous tempests, the movement at first

was little as a human hand. Hitler addressed, in his earliest speeches, tens, then scores, then hundreds, then thousands. It soon appeared that he had the demagogic arts in the fullest measure, and that people were in the mood to listen to him. Impartial observers were rarely able to detect a single sentence of distinct meaning in his enormously long orations; but they raised his susceptible audiences to an almost unheard-of pitch of enthusiasm. Every device of advertisement and propaganda was employed; bands, banners, slogans, repetitions, rhythmic croons. Amid the mass of verbiage, one thing was made plain, that Hitler was the Man, and that, like King Lear, he would do—what, he knew not yet, and his hearers did not know; but the very vagueness had its inspiration for the multitudes who felt that things were somehow all wrong but could not tell how they were wrong or what was the remedy. He gave them hope—and he gave them a scapegoat. Where a constructive plan was lacking, destructive plans were a useful substitute: destroy the Communist and destroy the Jew. That done, the malignant poison cleared out of the system, you will see!

At the first election, the Nazis, though they had gained vastly in numbers, were defeated: nor did they increase their power in the following months. But a strange paralysis had overtaken the Government; and Hindenburg, who was still great in prestige, did not support his own Ministers. Suddenly the Government offices were invaded, and, instead of sending for the police, the rulers surrendered on the spot—to a parcel of Junkers. As Mr. Mowrer has shrewdly said, the old habit of obedience was still strong in them; as the Mayor of Köpenick had obeyed a beggar dressed as a captain, so these men obeyed their "superiors". "They knew their place," and went out like dismissed butlers. Hindenburg appointed as Chancellor von Papen, who had distinguished himself during the war, when a member of the German Embassy in America, by stirring up trouble for the Americans, and talking of them as "idiotic Yankees", taking care to put down everything on papers which were duly captured by the British and published to the world.

Papen was only a stop-gap; and it was not long before he was quietly removed, and Hitler made Chancellor by the President. So soon as this happened, bands of Nazis appeared in the Government offices of all the subordinate States, and without meeting serious resistance established Nazi rule everywhere—which meant that the old semi-independence was at an end, and that Germany was now a totalitarian dominion. Even Bavaria, which had always prided itself on retaining a distinct character of its own, fell into the Nazi ranks with apparent eagerness: and Saxony, Baden, Württemberg, and the rest joined the common movement. What Bismarck had carefully refrained from attempting during thirty years was done in a few days by Hitler. Nor was this all. Nazis invaded Austria, and became, for many months, an extreme embarrassment to that unhappy country.

As for the Jews, their life had already been a burden. They were turned out of every post, banished, beaten, mobbed, killed: deprived of their means of livelihood, insulted, slandered. Thousands of the ablest men in the country emigrated, the illustrious Einstein among them; others were shut up in "Concentration Camps", to suffer atrocious tortures at the hands of brutal and fanatical warders.

The appointment of Hitler as Chancellor by the President was within the scope of the Constitution; and it might have been thought that the new " Leader " would have been content with it. But that, as we have seen, is rarely the way of dictators. They prefer to gain, by force or fraud, an apparent or real public confirmation of their position; and Hitler was no exception. An election must be held, and must be decisively won. But victory, even now, was by no means certain; and a narrow victory would be as bad as a defeat. A bogy and an election-cry were necessary, and the bogy must plainly be Communism. To the impartial eye the Communist menace was about as real as that of the Jews. Nothing, therefore, short of the most drastic action could convince the people at large that they need be afraid of it. A Catilinarian conspiracy, or a vast Gunpowder Plot, had therefore to be invented: and Goebbels, the Minister of Propaganda, was found equal to the task. One morning, early in 1932, the Reichstag was seen to be blazing: and the cry was heard all over Berlin that the Communists had been the incendiaries. An idiot Dutch youth had been seen lurking about the premises, and was obviously in Bolshevik pay. The news was diligently spread through the country: unless a strong Government was established the whole people might be burnt in their beds. Instantly there was a wild rush on everybody who was a Communist, who might be a Communist, or who had any connection with Communists. Arrests, beatings, shootings were to be seen everywhere.

At almost any other time, and in almost any other

country in the world the fantastic exaggerations would have roused ridicule, and would have provoked a strong reaction. Göring, Hitler's second in command, spoke of terrorist gangs who were to disguise themselves in " Stahlhelm " uniforms in order to murder right and left ; of poisonings by the thousand, of fires to be kindled all over the country : and Hitler followed with " revelations " of conspiracies intended to reduce civilisation everywhere to a mere heap of rubbish. Knowing how possible it is for a mob-orator to work himself up into believing anything whatever, we may perhaps admit that Hitler had persuaded himself that this contemptible rant was true : it at any rate seemed true to a people hypnotised with terror—as the tales of Titus Oates seemed true to people delirious with fear of the Popish Plot.

In this state of panic it might have seemed that no further stimulants were required : the result of the election was certain : but even so it was thought worth while to apply the methods which had been put to such successful use by Mussolini. It was as well to improve the blazing hour. Intimidation, chicanery, and fraud alternated with wild and irredeemable promises. The new constitution was approved, in consequence, by an overwhelming majority. Still more terrorism was accordingly justifiable ; opposition was now treason to the universal will ; and whosoever beat or pistolled an opponent of the Government was doing the nation service.

Shrewd people had seen at once something suspicious in the Reichstag fire. An investigation made in England, though imprudent in itself, brought many curious facts to light ; and a trial held some time later in Germany itself converted suspicion into practical certainty. A Bulgarian Communist, Dimitroff, accused of a share in the crime, distinguished himself by the vigour of his replies, and proved that he was in Bulgaria at the time; while Torgler, a German, was shown in the eyes of all foreigners as equally innocent. The poor Dutch idiot, though found guilty, was exhibited to the world as quite unequal to the task with which he was charged: and a simple deduction left only one conclusion possible; the fire had been deliberately contrived by Goebbels and his coadjutors as an electoral device. Dimitroff was perforce released; Torgler, though not found guilty, was sent back to the Concentration Camp, whence he never emerged: the lunatic — what did *his* life matter?—was executed as a futile proclamation to the world that some sort of justice had been done.

The Nazi programme had thus been fairly set on foot; and we may for a moment pause to mark the methods by which this preliminary end had been achieved. In appealing for support, reasoning had been carefully avoided; appeals had been made to the passions, and in particular to the passions of hate and fear: for it was felt that in an atmosphere of depression like that prevalent in Germany attention could not be gained without noise and excitement. Of all the passions hate and fear are the most easy to arouse, and the most likely to induce men to follow blindly a course prescribed for them by others. This is why, in a war, these feelings are deliberately stimulated by every known means; and a revolution is a form of war. In the absence of any real enemy, imaginary ones were set up; there already existed a dislike of the Jews and a fear of the Communists; it was not hard therefore to intensify these feelings, which, by a well-known law of nature, grow by being acted upon. From the very earliest times it has been perceived that we hate those we injure. And, as this feeling slowly dies down through sheer satiety, all sorts of violent stimulants must be administered: mass-psychology must be studied, armies must be paraded, drums must be beaten, flags must be waved. And everything must be concentrated on one man, whose praises must be constantly sung—with due observance of the moral of the old anecdote that Aristides must not be called the Just to a wearisome length. The eulogies must be varied and dexterous.

The frenzied cruelty with which " non-Aryans ", " half-breeds ", and Jews—whether Christian by religion or not—have been treated, and are still being treated, cannot be exaggerated, and for the mass of human misery thus caused we have to go back to the times of Attila and his Huns. The declared Jews have been reduced by emigration from about 600,000 to 400,000; but the number of " part-Aryans " cannot be counted; for intermarriage in happier days was exceedingly common, and no one is a full " Aryan " who cannot prove that neither of his grandparents was Jewish. No non-Aryan, whatever his religion, can be a civil servant, a judge, a teacher, or a professor; he cannot be a lawyer, a doctor, a journalist, a publisher; he cannot play in a public orchestra or theatre or picture-studio; nor may an " Aryan " firm take him on as an apprentice, or an Aryan hausfrau employ his daughter as a servant. Thus thrown out of employment, he may apply for unemployment relief, but he never receives it; an Aryan steppeth down before him. In any lawsuit he is doomed beforehand to failure, for it is a first principle of Nazi law that the rights of Aryans must be considered paramount to those of others.

In social intercourse things are if possible worse. An Aryan is forbidden to marry a Jew or half-Aryan, whether Christian or not; everybody must marry in his own caste. Divorces, broken engagements, suicides, untold misery, have been the consequences of this law. Legally, no Jewish child is permitted in a State school; and, though this regulation has been found impossible to keep with strictness, the plight of a child who does go to State schools is more pitiful than that of those who stay away. He cannot join in games, nor swim in the baths, nor join excursions, nor become one of the " Hitler Youth ", whose chances of good positions are always preferred. Doubtless, when these conditions have produced their inevitably degrading effect, the degradation will be used as an excuse for further insults.

Meanwhile, the streets are placarded by the fanatical Streicher with large-print lies—of which the insane story of ritual murder is the least disgusting and offensive. Fortunately, Streicher is said to have overreached himself. Familiarity has bred a just contempt, and the most purely Aryan citizens, we are told, now pass these monstrous advertisements without a glance. But it is too true that out of sight is out of mind. The Jews, and even the Christian Jews, have been forced into obscurity: indeed obscurity has been their only chance of life of any kind: and thus they have, it is true, escaped some tortures, but they have also ceased to arouse pity. The majority of decent Germans know nothing of the festering canker in their midst.*

How many would have supported Hitler at the beginning of his career if they had pondered on the common law of despotism, is hard to say. A slight acquaintance with history, and the application of it to their own case, might have acted as a warning. A tyrant's friendships are short-lived, and his earliest supporters are often the first to be discarded. Certainly the rule was not broken in the present instance. Among the chief supporters of Hitler was Hugenberg, a man of great influence both with financiers and with land-owners. Without his assistance it is practically certain that Hitler would never have been able to gain his place. So soon as the main opposition was crushed, Hugenberg was calmly thrust aside. Worse was to follow. In June 1934 disputes arose as to the reorganisation of the various armies in the Reich; and Hitler found, or suspected, that his own plans were not meeting with the approval of certain men, who had been among his closest friends and adherents. How far their designs went, no one knows : perhaps they did not know themselves. It does not seem probable that they actually aimed at the Leader's overthrow. At any rate he determined the " plots " should not mature, and acted with a decision and promptitude which, *per se*, were admirable. He went himself directly to the central point of disaffection, and faced his best friend, Röhm, in a small apartment. He did not arrest and try him. He shot him there and then : and at the same time, in

---

* These cruelties were, in their commencement, supported by falsified statistics as to the numbers of Jews in posts of importance. As a matter of fact, these numbers were never out of proportion : they were about one in a hundred of the total population.

different parts of the country, numbers of suspects—perhaps two hundred—were similarly put out of the way. Among these was General Schleicher, who had for a moment been chief man in the State, and who had in all probability taken no part in the movement. With him perished his wife, who was trying to protect him. These deeds appeared to the public not as murders, but as " executions "—though lacking even that farcical mimicry of a trial with which most tyrants like to delude the public.

It now began to be still more clearly revealed to the world that the nationalism preached by Hitler was more than ordinary patriotism, more even that the extraordinarily assertive Teutonism so visible before the war. Not only must all alien elements be cast out ; the State must set itself up as a deity to be worshipped, and must be proclaimed as such with a fanaticism worthy of early Moslem warriors. Long before, Hegel had personified the State, and contrived somehow to blend the million selves of its subjects into a single imperial ego : but this went even further. Each individual owed himself, his life, and his very thoughts to this intangible entity, of which the " Leader " was the representative and incarnation. Hitler, in fact, was a demigod, and his will was law and Gospel.

Not unnaturally, there were some who could not swallow a doctrine like this ; and those were to be found in the ranks of otherwise convinced Nazis. The Lutheran Church has always been remarkable, even among State Churches, for its close connection with the secular power ; but it was impossible for devout Christian pastors to forget the words, " We must obey God rather than man " ; and, to their eternal honour, great numbers of them faced the prospect of expulsion, indigence, and the concentration camp rather than yield on a point of conscience. A "Reichsbischoff" named Müller was found to undertake the task of compelling obedience; he utterly failed despite bluster, threats, and actual violence. A Remonstrance was read in many churches asserting that the dissidents, while loyal to the new régime in temporal affairs, must reserve the rights of conscience on the spiritual side.

As preached by Rosenberg, the leader of the Hitlerite religious movement, God was a German; and the conception of a unity among Christians throughout the world was anathema. Christianity, as generally understood, is tainted with Judaism, and the Jewish elements must be cast out. As Chamberlain had taught, Christ was not a Jew, and the fancy that his religion was of Jewish origin was a contemptible superstition, running directly contrary to Teutonic ideas. Still more, the "Christian" virtues—patience, forgiveness of injuries, humility—were unworthy of the proud and noble Germanic stock; we must return to Thor, Odin, and the old heroes, and substitute the Nibelungen Lied for the Acts of the Apostles. Let us commemorate these deities and demigods in place of the crawling and feeble objects of ecclesiastical reverence. Thus, and thus only, could the unity of Church and State be assured. Loyalty and worship would thus be one and undivided.

To this the nobler spirits opposed a firm resistance. They would have no return to Paganism. Under Pastor Niemöller they separated from the compliant National body, and formed a "Confessional Church" of their own, which so far has not been destroyed.

A similar and equally glorious courage has been shown

MODERN TYRANNIES 183

by the Catholic Church—the very name of which marks its insistence on its universality, and involves a denial that it can be limited by national boundaries. In some respects it has a stronger position than the Protestant Confession, for it has of course a vast power abroad, which it has used with considerable success. To its honour it has used this power not merely for itself, but on behalf of the persecuted heretics also. Here too the end is not yet: whether either Church will be able to resist for a generation or two the enormous pressure exerted in schools, in colleges, in the drilling-fields, and in daily contact with Nazi propagandism, time alone can tell. Already Hitler has done more than Bismarck himself was able to do; and he shows no sign of going to Canossa.

The pressure is indeed enormous; it is continuous, subtle, and all-pervasive. Wherever one goes one sees the swastika, the Nazi emblem: and no symbol which might by any possibility lessen its effect is allowed to flaunt itself. The old pleasant German salutation, "Grüss Gott", has all but died out in favour of "Heil Hitler". Enter the schools, and you hear a history, a geography, a natural science, all accommodated to Nazi ideas. Early in the war some Germans were said to have remarked, "When we have won, *we* shall write the story of its origin, its battles, and its results." They did not win, but they are writing the story, and a fantastic one it is; but no contradiction is ever allowed, and the pupils believe it all. The biological lessons teach the children the Nazi fiction of an "Aryan" race, to which they belong. "Spartam nactus es," every one is taught; "hanc exorna". All this is under the control of an officer of State, who appoints the masters, watches them remorselessly, and dismisses them if they fall short of his requirements. Similarly with music, painting, statuary. The first demand from a candidate for any scholastic post is not capacity but obedience: and every effort is made that the rising generation may be impregnated with a strong delusion, to believe a lie.

All this might be observed from other countries with interest but without terror, as a remarkable experiment in the moulding of a great people, if part, and a very important part, of the system were not the cultivation of military habits, and the deliberate fostering of national hatreds. It is possible to look on with approval as Germany recovers her self-respect under the leadership of " a man sent from God "; and many have been quite willing to see the Saar restored, even by a vote not quite free, to its proper place. One can understand, also, the German feeling of triumph when, by a daring act, at a moment skilfully chosen, the Rhine provinces were refortified. But this is one thing: the perpetual boastings of military strength as the mark of national greatness, and the provocations of foreign countries, are another. At the very time when Russia, under Stalin, has announced her renunciation of Bolshevik propaganda outside her own territory, and has shown herself more peacefully inclined than ever before, a series of furious denunciations is launched against her, not only by newspapers and subordinate ministers but by Hitler himself: and the whole world is thrown into a state of feverish anxiety worse than that which heralded the outbreak of 1914. At the same time, with the sensitiveness which so often marks the master of flouts and jeers, he resents much milder attacks upon himself, and complains of caricatures such as, among free peoples, ministers are accustomed to endure from their own countrymen. Whether he actually desires war or not is doubtful ; amid all these inflammatory utterances he constantly proclaims his desire for peace ; but it is certain that his methods are precisely those best adapted for bringing on war.

The state of feeling in a country under these influences is hard for those outside to realise. Even English Liberals, returning from a visit to Germany—where the word has gone round that they are to be effusively welcomed—have confessed that they have found it difficult to resist the atmosphere, and that it takes time for them to throw off the glamorous influence. The hopeful look on the faces of those one meets, the adoration of the Leader which appears everywhere, and which is plainly a sincere and rooted feeling, is specially striking to those who saw the depression a few years since. It is like clear shining after rain. There are, it is true, signs here and there that the unity is not absolute. A chauffeur, driving a foreigner to his hotel, after first making sure that he cannot be overheard, will ask eagerly, " Is there a chance of work for me in your country ? " and one may see, occasionally, a broken man who has been purposely released from a concentration camp as a visible proof of what happens to enemies of the Nazi system. But such things are rare. It is possible to live long in the country and notice nothing but a well-ordered people, marching with one mind to a goal which they do not descry, but which they are sure must be the right one since the Leader has chosen it. No shocks can move this simple faith. A few venturesome strangers have, at times, ventured to question some of the demigod's actions. They have invariably received the answer, worthy of an old saint perplexed by the ways of Providence, " It can't be wrong, because He did it."

Some refugees, with the sanguine expectations which exiles so often harbour, look forward to the fall of Hitler: but so far there is nothing to show the decline of his popularity : and every year, of course, strengthens the system he has founded. He may die, and then there may be a struggle for his place, and true men may have a chance of coming by their own ; but apart from some unpredictable accident or some disastrous war, it seems at present as if the world must be prepared to face the problem of Nazi Germany, moved machine-like by one will, and ready to accept caprice as an oracular command. It may well be, also, that Nazism or Fascism may obtain such a hold in half the countries of the world that even if destroyed in one place it may still flourish in others.

It may be interesting here to recall the words used in 1860, to characterise the despotism of Napoleon, by a German historian.

" External trade was of course extinct : in its place industry was devoted to such luxuries as silk, gold, glass. Where it was still possible to employ the labouring classes, their energies were set to the making of roads, houses, or imposing buildings, remarkable rather for their colossal size than for beauty. As for the sciences, the mathematical flourished, but history and philosophy were dead : and the reason is plain : they were the victims of the suppression of individual independence and personal liberty. The lycées, from 1808 onwards, received their teaching staffs from the Imperial University, which was under military control. The elementary schools were of little account; but their main purpose was the inculcation of the duty of obedience to authority. The rising generation was to receive the stamp of a single domineering mind.

"It was enough for Napoleon if he could ask with confidence, Is there a man who can lead armies, manage finance, organise law and police? He failed to see that this does not touch the kernel of human nature. In every man, in every people, dwells a *personality*, expressing itself in speech and custom, in free assent and dissent, in attractions and repulsions, which is rooted in recollections of childhood and in attachment to the home, which drives one man abroad and chains another to his hearthstone, which gives the directive impulse to everyone's special vocation, to law, to the State, and to the popular religion. Of all this Napoleon had no conception."

One wonders what Heinrich von Sybel, who saw so clearly the defects of the Napoleonic régime, would have thought of the Hitlerian system had he lived to see it.

A short account is necessary of a man whom I hesitate, in the absence of decisive information, to call a tyrant, or even a dictator, though for two years he wielded dictatorial powers, and indeed assumed them with hardly the slightest show of legality. I would rather rank him with Oliver Cromwell, who in my opinion took power reluctantly, and under the conviction that he was sent by God to bring order to a distracted country, or with Julius Cæsar, who— as many scholars believe—was driven against his will to make himself sole ruler of the Roman world. Be these comparisons fair or not, the man of whom I am about to speak used his authority with some moderation, made efforts to share it, and seems to have been inspired by a real love of his country. Though on one occasion he shed blood—and then, as many hold, unwillingly—he ordered no proscriptions, issued amnesties, permitted political opponents to live peaceably if they would, and—allowance being made for the almost intolerable difficulties of his position—may perhaps go down to posterity with Pittacus, the "Æsymnete" of Mitylene.* He died poor, after having done his best to enrich his people.

Of all the mistakes of the Allies, not the least fatal was their treatment of Austria. Before the war, the two realms of Austria and Hungary contained about fifty million people, of a dozen different nationalities, uneasily kept together under a single crown. The chief city, Vienna, one of the greatest ornaments of the world, reckoned about two millions. By the Peace of Saint Germain, more than six-sevenths of the population of the Dual Monarchy were torn away; and immediately the newly-formed dominions set up impassable tariff-walls against the diminished State, which was forbidden to rectify its financial position by so much as a Zollverein with Germany. Here then was a country with a capital holding one-third of its people, unable to export goods abroad, with starvation ever at hand, and with a currency debased till it was not worth the paper on which the so-called values were printed. The days of barter returned. Not unnaturally, Socialism, Communism, Anarchism found here a fruitful breeding-

* Mr. J. D. Gregory's *Life of Dollfuss* must be read with caution; his picture is certainly too favourable.

ground : and extremists of all kinds received daily recruits. Despair, and consequent recklessness, were rampant.

The Emperor Karl had fled, and a Socialist Republican Government was established, which, as was inevitable, could not govern. Although no other government, in such circumstances, could have done better, it was natural that the existing ministry should be blamed for the troubles by those who had, in their sufferings, lost the ability to form clear judgments. There was a constant succession of Cabinets, each as helpless as its predecessor. At length an able and, so far as can be seen, upright priest, Monsignor Seipel, gained some semblance of power, and contrived—at a price—to induce the League of Nations to stabilise the currency and assist the shattered finances by a loan. This was an immense service : men who had found a nominal income of two hundred English pounds worth about seven shillings now discovered that they had the equivalent of fifteen shillings per annum. Seipel, whose idea was to make some working arrangement between the Church and the moderate Socialists, might now expect some slight general improvement ; but desperation had now gone too far, and violence had become a habit. Seipel was attacked by a frantic Socialist and dangerously wounded ; an incident which did not tend to cement the very loose connections between the Church party and the multitudinous contending factions ; and the Socialists, unfortunately, were in possession of arms, some recently manufactured, but most of them skilfully hidden away at the conclusion of the war. Among the Socialists themselves there was little agreement, save in the one point of dislike of the Government ; and throughout the country there were thousands of Ishmaelites who were against everybody else, and against whom everybody's hand was ready to strike.

The strength of the Government and its clerical friends lay in the peasantry, a sturdy and independent class of men, from whom, in the main, was formed the Heimwehr, or Home Defence Force, a militia not fully disciplined, but capable of vigorous action. To a certain extent, also, the regular army (limited by the Peace to thirty thousand men) could be relied on; and the police, on the whole, were a tolerably competent, united, loyal, and well-managed body. Given time, the Government might have been able to establish order. But the opponents were at least as powerful. Seitz, the Mayor—and the mayors in Continental cities are important officers—was a Socialist, commanded a workers' militia, and took little pains to keep his party in hand. During the Socialist administration, at ruinous expense, great industrial homes had been built which were practically fortresses, were honeycombed with secret passages, and were packed with munitions. Of these the Karl-Marx-Hof was only the most famous; half the suburbs had similar citadels, some planted in commanding positions.

Ere long there was added a great and terrible menace. The Nazis were rising in Germany, and made no secret of their design to treat Austria as a German province. They crossed the border in bands, murdered and terrorised in all directions, and formed alliances with native Austrians of similar mentality. Thus the Government had to fight on two fronts, while they were harassed by crowds of unattached snipers, and were not too certain of the loyalty of their nominal supporters.

In the midst of all this Seipel, whose health was never robust, and who had never fully recovered from his wound, died; and after a short and insignificant interval a remarkable man took his place. Engelbert Dollfuss was a peasant by birth, and retained his peasant sympathies to the end. He was a devout Catholic, but he had the advantage that at least he was not in orders. He had served under Seipel as Minister of Railways, and by his personal charm had gained the affection of the railwaymen, a fact of great importance in what was to come. He had then become Minister of Agriculture, and had, if that were possible, strengthened his hold upon the peasantry. But his great asset was his size, which was the reverse of gigantic, and was the joy of innumerable caricaturists. He was credited with a ladder for climbing into bed, and was caricatured as Gulliver, chased by puppy-dogs, among the Brobdingnagians. There was nothing about him of the imposing dwarfishness of Napoleon; but it was gradually discovered that he had much of Napoleon's force of will, and that his endearing smile hid fixed purpose. It was therefore a wise, though unexpected, step when in May, 1932, President Miklas appointed him Chancellor.

It was, said Miklas, to be a Ministry of Personalities; and Dollfuss, to the best of his ability, acted on the advice. He chose, as chief of the Heimwehr, Prince Starhemberg, the heir of an "Apostolic" family of almost mythical antiquity, and a direct descendant of the hero who, in 1683, held Vienna against the Turks, until it was relieved by John Sobieski. Starhemberg was a popular leader, but impulsive and inconsistent. Justice was in the hands of Dr. Schuschnigg, a lawyer of distinction; and the budget was given to an able financier named Kienböck. There were other men in the Government; but for a time almost the whole of the work was done by Dollfuss himself.

Even with perfect peace that work would have been crushing: but there was, in effect, civil war. The Nazis, since Hitler's rise to supreme power in Germany, were more aggressive, violent, and murderous than ever. Nothing could exceed their violence and fanaticism. Hitler had already, in dividing Germany into thirty-three departments, marked down Austria as one of them; and the Nazis habitually acted as if the country were their own, and as if therefore all who opposed them were, like Jews and Communists in Prussia and Bavaria, traitors to be exterminated without mercy. They were everywhere, and stuck at no atrocity: nor was it possible to prevent their invasions, the number of passes into the country being too great for the Heimwehr to defend. It is probable, however, that the Nazis defeated their own purpose. The desire for the *Anschluss* or incorporation into Germany had already died down; and Nazi antagonism to the Church, not to speak of other causes, hourly alienated Austrian feeling more and more. On this, at any rate, Socialists were at one with the Catholic party.

As one means of protecting himself against this cloud of locusts, Dollfuss sought the dangerous friendship of Mussolini, who, it was well known, would never permit Germany to reach the Alps. This policy exposed the Chancellor to much obloquy, and to the charge that his sympathies were really Fascist. But it is probable that he was quite sincere in his announcement that he came to provide peace and unity for the people. He certainly offered posts in his Government to Socialists, and called himself a Socialist—with the significant addition of the word " Christian ". Faction, however, was too deeply rooted. The opposition meant to oppose, and nothing else. At the election which followed his accession to the Chancellorship he gained a majority of *one*: and in the subsequent debates, there was confusion and uproar which, to him, meant that the Parliamentary system was unworkable. He therefore determined to rule without a Parliament. As he left the Chamber, he said " Never again."

It is here that we meet an irreconcilable clash of opinions. A man who cries for national unity, when unity means submission to himself, is always suspect: and Dollfuss only suffers the inevitable fate of the saviour of society who claims to be the personified nation. Socialists say, probably with truth, that he had no majority in the country: the supporters of Dollfuss answer that, however this might be, his party was larger than any one of the warring factions which opposed him, and which combined only to make his rule impossible.

There is even more keen dispute as to the event which followed. It was of course known that the Socialists had arms; it was suspected that they meditated a *coup d'état*—though this again has been passionately denied. A search for arms was ordered; the usual " incidents " happened; some of the police were shot; and the rebellion was either provoked or deliberately and wantonly started, according to the predilections of observers. One point in favour of the Socialist view is that the rising, real or imaginary, was so easily crushed. In a few days it was over : and the casualties were comparatively few. But the material destruction was great : it was impossible to destroy the fortress of Karl-Marx-Hof without destroying the splendid workers' dwellings which it included ; and Dollfuss has never been forgiven, in some quarters, for this act of—as we please—either vandalism or military necessity. In other respects he was, as Dictators go, merciful : not many of the " rebels " were hanged, and a proclamation of amnesty was speedily issued, once again with an appeal for unity. The State was to be Christian, but full liberty of thought was to be permitted ; Jews, Protestants, and utter unbelievers might share its beneficial activities. It was hinted that the dictatorship was but temporary ; so soon as order was restored, Dollfuss would gladly retire. Here again he was, possibly, sincere : but unluckily the same sort of thing has been said by almost every dictator, and the wolf's cry that he is only a sheep is not now easy to trust.

Even if he was in truth guilty, the vengeance came from the wrong quarter. His life had been attempted already once by a Nazi, who fortunately was a poor performer with the pistol ; and he received threatening letters every day. Worse still, his children were menaced with the fate of the Lindbergh baby. At last the threats came to fruition. Rintelen, whom he had sent as ambassador to Rome, perhaps to be under the watchful eye of Mussolini, was a Nazi, and from his Italian vantage-ground carried on intrigues with his Nazi friends. The Chancellor was to be secretly murdered ; and it was to be announced that, though alive and well, he had proclaimed Rintelen as his successor. Rintelen took his holiday in Vienna, to be ready for the expected blow. On July 25, 1934, a band of Nazis drove up to the Ballplatz, overpowered the guards, and accomplished their purpose. They then seized Major Fey, the war-minister, and at the pistol-point compelled him to announce that Dollfuss had resigned in Rintelen's favour. There was naturally some confusion in the counsels of the people; but happily there was still more confusion, and indeed inconceivable stupidity, among the murderers. They were soon compelled to surrender: Rintelen, after vainly trying to kill himself, was arrested in the hotel where he was waiting the news; and the attempt, apart from the one fatal result, was a dismal fiasco. Meanwhile, Dollfuss lay slowly dying; with callous brutality the murderers denied him both a doctor and a priest. He named Schuschnigg as his successor.

No sooner did Mussolini hear of the murder than he hastened to offer his sympathy to Madame Dollfuss. Doubtless he said, as he had said to Madame Matteotti, that he wished he could recall her husband from the grave. But *this* time his sympathy and his indignation were intense and genuine; for a friend of his, and not an enemy, had been murdered. To overawe the Nazis, who, both in Austria and Germany, were becoming active, he moved forty thousand troops to the border; and this had its effect. There is no doubt, also, that many of Dollfuss's opponents were revolted by the murderous method of settling quarrels. The death of the Chancellor thus accomplished more than he might have achieved in years of life; from that moment the power of Naziism declined.

Schuschnigg was expected to be a mere stop-gap; and in fact for many months his colleague Starhemberg was generally imagined to be the ruling partner. There were the usual insanities of despotism, among them a censorship of literature and of the press. A list of banned books of which the *New Statesman* (Oct. 16, 1936) gave a selection, shows the sort of thing which a nominally liberal Catholic-Social government thinks it undesirable for its citizens to read. The *index expurgatorius* includes *Utopia*, Siegfried's *English Crisis*, and books by Gorki, Gandhi, Lloyd George, Dostoeffsky, Bertrand Russell, Masaryk, Freud, Wells, and Sidney and Beatrice Webb. More remarkably, it includes *Pan-Europa*, an attack on Russian Bolshevism, and the *Last Days of Mankind* by Karl Kraus, an admirer of Dollfuss. The entire freedom of thought which Dollfuss promised seems already to have vanished from the programme.

The latest, but by no means the last, incident in the warfare has been the dismissal of Starhemberg; for it has turned out that Schuschnigg is not the cipher he was thought to be. Taking advantage of a quarrel between Starhemberg and Major Fey, he skilfully manipulated his council until he had induced the Prince's chief supporters to abandon him. He then announced the dissolution not merely of the Heimwehr, Starhemberg's special force, but also of every other arm except one, which was to be the State "defensive force", to absorb the trusty elements of the rest, and to swear allegiance to the Chancellor alone. This done, he calmly flew off to attend the funeral of General Gömbös, the Hungarian dictator. Starhemberg, apparently weary and indifferent, made a feeble resistance; and went quietly into retirement. He seems content with the contemplation of his splendid ancestry and the enjoyment of his estates. He is not likely to make any effort to return. What the policy of the new autocrat will be can only be guessed: but it will probably not be one of greater freedom. There are hints, vague and cautious, that the Hapsburgs may be restored. There are more than hints that the censorship of the press is to be retained; and where the press is muzzled Governments are tyrannical.

These tyrannies may show every shade of political or social belief; they may be Nazi, Fascist, Communist, or anything you please; but they are all alike in one point. All have openly avowed that justice is with them a matter of political opinion. Law is one thing for the supporters of the régime, another for opponents. In England—at least theoretically—the administrators of the law are supposed to be free from party bias, and to deal "indifferent justice" to peer, peasant, Tory, Liberal, Radical, or Socialist: in countries under these modern dictatorships not only is the reverse the case in practice, but it is ostentatiously proclaimed as the theory also. Hence some of the most astounding mockeries of justice since the days of Titus Oates. The trial of the murderers of Matteotti was a self-confessed farce, in which no reference was allowed to those who had ordered the crime, and no attempt to trace it to its origin was permitted. At Bologna in 1926, a shot was fired in the midst of a crowd which was acclaiming Mussolini. A boy named Zamboni was instantly seized, and killed without trial. It was certain that he had not fired the shot; it was not certain that the cartridge was not blank. But, as it was considered necessary to show the world that Mussolini's life was not to be attempted with impunity, and as it would have been impolitic to seem to admit that an innocent boy had been put to death, a mock-trial was held. Zamboni's father, who had been an Anarchist in his youth, but had long been a professed Fascist, was sentenced to thirty years' imprisonment; the boy's aunt, who had carried a revolutionary flag in a procession twenty years before, received the same sentence; and an endeavour was made to prove that the shot was really fired by Zamboni's brother Lodovico. Lodovico was able to show that he had been all the time in Milan, undergoing military training. No matter—the State required *some* victim, innocent or guilty; and Lodovico was condemned to five years' detention in the penal islands.

Parallels to this could easily be found in Russia or Germany. Even in Austria, under the comparatively mild Schuschnigg, who has disclaimed the title of dictator, persons are arrested by the police, and sentenced, *by the police*, without trial, to months of imprisonment. Mere suspicion is enough. Often, when a "legal" trial has been undergone, and sentence passed and served, the police increase it. Amnesties have been proclaimed—and curious exceptions have been made: certain men still remain, somehow, in prison, though officially set at liberty.

Yet there are people, in England, who defend a state of things in which *they themselves*, if it suited the Government, might be packed off to Lampedusa without a shred of evidence against them. The "good of the State" would demand the sacrifice, and they would have to submit.

CONCLUSION

"I well remember that, when the examples of former Jacobins, as Julius Cæsar, Cromwell, and the like, were adduced in France and England, at the commencement of the French Consulate, it was ridiculed as pedantry and pedants' ignorance to fear a repetition of usurpation and military despotism at the close of the *enlightened eighteenth century*. The magi of the day gave us set proofs that similar results were impossible, and that it was an insult to so philosophical an age, to so enlightened a nation, to dare direct the public eye towards them as lights of warning."—*Samuel Taylor Coleridge*.

No dictum is more famous, and none has been more utterly stultified by the event, than that of President Wilson—"We must make the world safe for democracy". The conflict entered upon with that sanguine expectation has so far had the opposite effect. From China to Portugal a chain of despotisms has been forged, and its weaker links seem to be constantly strengthening. Where there was autocracy before, as in Turkey, Russia, and Germany, a more powerful autocracy has been set up; and where there was constitutional liberty, real or pretended, it has been ruthlessly crushed. In the countries which still retain freedom, there is serious fear that it may be suppressed; and there are, in almost every country, organisations aiming, openly or furtively, at its suppression.

That Wilson, a trained historian, should have uttered the saying, and have been convinced that it would justify itself, is somewhat surprising; for all history shows that long wars are dangerous, if not fatal, to democratic institutions. The very first word spoken by a Liberal historian after the declaration of war in 1914 was, " This will be the death of Liberalism " : and he gave a dozen examples to explain his fear. In 287 B.C. the laws of Hortensius made Rome a democracy. The Punic Wars followed ; and Rome emerged a tyrannical oligarchy, which, after a hundred years of unrest, gave way, not to democracy, but to the rule of military dictators. During the Napoleonic war, the Liberal members of our own Parliament could be conveyed in two hackney-carriages ; and when the war was over, seventeen years passed before Liberalism recovered. On the Continent, things were worse ; the Holy Alliance made people regret Napoleon, and wish that Waterloo had gone otherwise. Too soon the historian's prophecy proved true. To win the war we had, or fancied we had, to give up many of our much-prized liberties, which we have not yet entirely regained. Dora was an unconscionable time in dying.

It was therefore no matter for wonder that the upheaval of the war should, in countries less accustomed to freedom than ours, lead to the establishment of despotisms ; the only wonder is that they were not established earlier. The confusion, physical distress, and mental unrest which prevailed even in the so-called " victorious " countries, and still more in the vanquished ones, were a natural breeding-ground for trust in a deliverer who should promise the people some remission of their evils. A bold and self-confident man might easily, at such a time, assume the character of a Messiah ; and in Turkey such a man appeared almost at once in the person of Mustapha Kemal. In other countries attempts at setting up a despotism, Red or White, were made ; but it would appear that they were made by the wrong men, preaching the wrong doctrines. Usually, the misery of the populace was too complete for them even to take means to escape from it. The patient had to recover to a certain extent before he would call in a doctor, quack or genuine as accident might determine. But call him in, sooner or later he would: and he generally found the doctor waiting at the door. Once let in, the physician had the invalid at his mercy, and proceeded to make himself indispensable, to get rid of rival practitioners, and to represent his own school of medicine as the only sound one. His position, in fact, enabled him easily to put out of the way any invalid who should show an inclination to call in another doctor. Unquestionably there would be many who would thrive under his treatment, and would be only too glad to sing the praises of their physician.

There is no doubt that there is some comfort in submission to confident authority, and in being saved the necessity of making a choice. Where there is but one candidate in a constituency, the elector is spared the trouble of going to the poll, or what is often the worse trouble of weighing the competing claims: and it is on this feeling that the would-be despot largely relies, and relies with success. The disadvantages of despotism are not felt till later; and too frequently the terrible result is brought about that they are not felt at all. It is hard to recall freedom once lost, and as the poet says,

" . . . dreadful truth it is that men
Forget the heaven from which they fall."

But the question of real importance to *us* is, " Can it

happen here?" a question which has been powerfully put even in the land of Washington and Jefferson. The anxiety is natural, and healthy : for the price of freedom is eternal vigilance. The approaches of tyranny are silent and crafty, and its final spring is often totally unexpected. It finds its opportunity most easily not in the activities of its open supporters but in the apathy and blindness of its enemies. And it is to be feared that there is among us in Britain much of this blindness and apathy. There are as yet few Fascists who hanker after Italian methods, and few Communists who would like to imitate Lenin. But there are multitudes of indifferentists, a class of people who, as that good Liberal Augustine Birrell said, are much worse than the most reactionary of Tories; who, like Dr. Johnson, would not give five shillings to live under one government rather than under another; whose only force is that of inertia, and who will submit to anything if resistance means effort. Above all, they hate the effort of thought; and, in Milton's words, they "love bondage more than liberty; bondage with ease than strenuous liberty", especially when it is strenuous thinking that the emergency demands. There are others who take no precautions because they are confident that the thing cannot come : those who utter warnings, they say, are crying Fire in Noah's Flood. The British character, they think, is a sufficient assurance that we shall never surrender our liberties. It has taken much time and much blood to secure them, and we have not forgotten : freedom is now almost a second nature, a character inherited like our features from our fathers. As well expect our faces to go negroid as our liberties to vanish. But it is precisely in this confidence that danger may lurk. Already, if we are to believe certain very eminent legal authorities, much of our control over our rights has been quietly pilfered from us by the bureaucrats of the Civil Service ; and there is no reason to believe that the pilfering is not still going on. And, if we look back at the history of the despotic movements in other countries, we shall see that there, only shortly before the great change took place, there was the same unsuspiciousness in the general public. No one, a year or two before Hitler or Mussolini seized power, had any real hope or fear of either. Their day came suddenly, like a thief in the night. To use words applied to a scarcely more violent catastrophe, " When people arose in the morning, behold, they were all dead corpses." If we too sleep, something similar may come upon us.

If, then, autocracy does come, it will be our own fault, and it behoves all who value liberty to be prepared. There are two kinds of danger, external and internal. We may be overcome by foreign force ; and the blindness to this peril is one of the most amazing phenomena of the time. If the British Empire is an expression of liberty, and if the Tory party is, as it claims to be, the guardian of the Empire, it is surprising that its leaders and its rank and file should not perceive that the cause it has been pursuing is precisely the one best adapted for destroying that Empire. Control of the Mediterranean is absolutely vital to our " imperial " interests ; but our Government, till facts could no longer be blinked, looked on while the Mediterranean was gradually, but rapidly, being transformed into a Fascist lake. Government organs have hardly concealed their sympathy with the Spanish insurgents; and amid all the charges and counter-charges, the assertions and denials, it is at any rate clear that the insurgents have been supplied—at a price—with Fascist and Nazi munitions of war, without which they would have been helpless. Italian troops—according to trustworthy witnesses—have occupied Majorca, and Italian and German aeroplanes have been seen by impartial observers assisting rebel armies. This aid the rebels have not been able to purchase with money; the *quid pro quo* is a matter of suspicion. Franco has emphatically denied that any cession of territory has been so much as mentioned; and he may be telling the truth. But there must be some entente with the friendly Powers; some promise of help in the attainment of the great aim—a Fascist hegemony in Europe. Mussolini boasts of his eight million soldiers: and Hitler is at least equally emphatic. In a short time, at the present rate, the two will have received a vast accession of strength, not merely in numbers but—what is more important—in strategic position. Nor must it be forgotten that mercury is the chief ingredient of explosives, and that Spain possesses the most productive mercury mines in the world. It is thought by some, indeed, that it is for these mines that the civil war has been stirred up.

Against this terrible invasion, which, in the almost religious fanaticism of its soldiers, recalls rather the Mohammedan peril of the seventh and eighth centuries than the Napoleonic menace which scared our ancestors, there is but one safeguard—" collective security ". It is a movement which combines the patient and secret enthusiasm of the Jesuits with more than the material force of the Armada : and it must be resisted as that was resisted—" only more so ": for that invasion was overcome too largely by the aid of chance or Providence. Had the League of Nations not been betrayed by its own chief members, the machinery for such collective security would have been ready to hand ; the machinery will have to be manufactured anew. If this work is speedily, honestly, and resolutely undertaken and carried through, the external danger will be less formidable. Here it is satisfactory to be assured that practically all parties in the country are agreed. Whether it may not be found that the horse has been stolen before the stable-door has been shut, is another question.

But perhaps still more necessary than these precautions, which it is the part of the Governments to take, is the watch the ordinary citizen must keep over his own thoughts It is easy for us to become impatient with the slowness inseparable from democratic institutions. A system which allows debate is inevitably less rapid than one in which opposition is forbidden ; and all of us have felt irritation when a course we think obviously right is obstructed by some obstinate talker. We contrast the state of things with that in which a ruler gives his orders and they are obeyed. The difference is of course most obvious in war-time. Had Marlborough enjoyed the authority of Napoleon, the twelve years' war of the Spanish succession would probably have been over in a few months ; and conversely, had Alexander been a constitutional monarch, he might never have conquered Persia. But it is equally present, though less visibly, in times of peace. Reforms which a despot, if so inclined, can bring about by a stroke of the pen, often take years in England, and even when effected, are often so much emasculated by the compromises and exceptions which have been necessary to conciliate opponents, as to lose half their advantages. One example out of hundreds is enough. It took endless toil to destroy the slave-trade; Alexander II abolished serfdom in a day.

It is of the utmost importance that we should face this issue fairly, and make up our minds about it. Is freedom worth this price—certainly a heavy one ? On our answer to this question—and not merely on our answer to it but on our feeling about it—depends our future. We must not only be *logically* convinced: our conviction must become part and parcel of our whole mental and moral make-up : or some morning we shall wake and behold we shall be dead corpses. We must become as determined believers in our system as the young men and women of Germany are believers in Hitlerism or those of Russia in Communism.

Fortunately, if we can be content with long views, if we can look ahead and have an eye to the future rather than to the immediate present, the decision between the two systems will be easily made. Nay, if we take a wide and comprehensive survey of the past, we shall come to the same conclusion. We must not press too far John Stuart Mill's assertion, that the ideally best polity is representative government. There are countries and times not fit for it. But it is incontrovertible that in countries which have once learned to apply representative institutions no other form is in any way satisfactory. To those who are inclined to doubt, I would recommend a calm perusal of Mill's book.

To the opinion that, if a good despot could be found, despotic government would be the best, Mill answers that even if such a despot could be found—and the very nature of despotism is to corrupt the despot—we have to find an all-seeing one. He must not only mean well, but must have the eyes of Argus multiplied ten thousand times. He must be a Haroun Al-Raschid with his curiosity and vigour in myriad measure. But assume that we do find this omniscient and morally perfect being. We then have a single man of superhuman powers managing a passive people. Their passivity is implied in the very idea of absolute power; all is decided for them and not by them; and it is a crime to resist. What sort of people will be formed under such a " monstrous regiment " ? Their intellectual activities are limited to a few sciences or arts not likely to be dangerous to the ruler ;* only a small class will be permitted to apply their powers either to inventions with a military purpose, or to training for the bureaucracy. Even religion will be diverted to so-called patriotic ends, or will narrow into a secret personal affair between the individual and his Maker. Apart from those few studious men who love speculation or knowledge for its own sake, the intelligence of the nation will be devoid of material interests. There

* I well remember observing in Russia, after the suppression of the revolt of the Intelligentsia in 1905, how these most highly cultured people, denied the chance of influencing politics, devoted themselves to music, painting, or mathematics. But even these were watched by authority. The police were always present as jealous censors, at the opera or the play : and one might almost say, with some exaggeration, that the very chess-players felt themselves under supervision.

CONCLUSION

is not a single example in all history of a nation which has given way to despotic rule without intellectually or morally degenerating. And this degeneration begins at once, even when the despot shows some approach to the character of a " good " one.

A " good " despotism means a government in which, so far as the despot is concerned, there is no positive oppression by the Officers of State, but in which the collective affairs of the people are managed for them, in which the political thinking is done apart from them, and in which their minds are formed by, and consent to, this abdication of their energies. How is it possible for such a people to avoid degeneration ? With the best side of their minds in abeyance, they inevitably suffer a gradual, but accelerating, decline in all their powers. A non-political people becomes a non-intellectual people: as, conversely, a people alive to politics invariably shows energy in all the functions of life. Contrast the vigour of Athens after the expulsion of Peisistratus with its apathy under his rule; and you will say, with Herodotus, " Freedom is a good thing". Contrast the vitality of Florence in its republican days with its sluggishness under the later Medici, and you will, with Barbour, "think Freedom more to prize than all the gold in world that is".

Imagine, again, a country which has no voice as to the tremendous issue of peace or war. It is true that, even in democracies, Governments have a considerable power of disguising those issues, and of so presenting their case that the people may be deceived into thinking an unjust and unnecessary war a righteous and unavoidable one. But the rulers have at least to make *some* case, and they have to meet reasoned opposition to it ; nor do they dare to go to war, which has to be fought by the people, without, by some means, gaining the people's consent. There are many who blamed Wilson for waiting so long before forcibly resenting the aggressions of Germany. But there is no doubt that, by thus waiting, he carried with him a practically united nation, and intervened with far greater effect than if he had dragged an unwilling multitude into the adventure. Similarly, our own Government in 1914 did not move until Germany, by the violation of Belgium, had made a great people " one voice around a King *advancing* to his wars." In a despotically-ruled country, on the other hand, the word of the despot must be blindly obeyed, a pretext, false or genuine, must be accepted at his will, and millions must go to be slaughtered because one man has determined their death. That their consent *seems* voluntary only makes matters worse. All the arts of advertisement, demagogy, and cajolery have been used to secure an ignorant and infantile credulity.

These are only a few of the advantages we, and the inhabitants of other free countries possess, and which some loud-voiced orators wish us to forgo. Let me mention another, which I may sum up in one phrase. We have the privilege of being able to " write to *The Times* " ; and, whether *The Times* prints our lucubrations or not, the mere act of putting pen to paper is a satisfaction. It blows off steam both for the Colonel in the club and for the pacifist in the street. Ever since " Jacob Omnium ", a hundred years ago, discovered this method of ventilating imaginary or real grievances, it has been used daily by hundreds of people, and has emphatically " done them good". But nothing of the kind is possible in a Fascist country. A man with a grievance is discontented with his rulers; he is therefore a traitor; and he will be lucky if he is not shipped off to a penal island. Let this fact be borne in mind by all who sigh for a one-man rule—a democratic country is the only one in which the individual can grumble as he will; where he can say what he thinks of the arrogance of Tite Barnacle, of the stupidity of a Cabinet Minister, of the dilatoriness of the Town Council, of the impertinence of the telephone officials. What the right of grumbling means, especially to an Englishman, he hardly realises now, for it is part of his inheritance. He would realise it the instant he was deprived of it. Nor, of course, though unreasonable grumbling has its value, is by any means all grumbling unreasonable. There are innumerable genuine grievances which ought, and need, to be proclaimed abroad; and the people to proclaim them are those who feel them; for it is astonishing how insensible we are to other people's troubles: we never notice them until we are compelled to notice them by main force. No one knows where the shoe pinches but the man who wears it; and a country in which it is impossible to publish one's vexations must, in time, harbour a vast amount of discontent, which may suddenly break out to the discomfiture of the rulers. For some months or years the feeling of the people may be swallowed up in a certain enthusiasm for the leader who has bewitched them, or in the excitement of an adventure into which he has drawn them; but a chronic and silent uneasiness will subsist, and, having no safety-valve, will be ready to show itself, when opportunity arises, in portentous form.

Let the reader consider for a moment a few of the other privileges, which he enjoys, and of which he would be deprived the very instant a Fascist government was imposed. He may, so long as he confines himself to peaceful methods, proclaim any doctrine, political, religious, or scientific, which he may adopt. He may address an audience—if he can get one—in Hyde Park, and describe the blessings of Communism. He may attack the present Government to his heart's content, and the police will see that he is not stoned or beaten by his opponents. He may, in this monarchical country, extol Republicanism. He may even, with perfect freedom, defend that very Fascism which, if it ever got the power, would deny freedom to others. Sir Oswald Mosley, if only he refrains from violence, may hire a hall and tell the Socialists that, if he becomes a Mussolini, he will not allow them to criticise him. An atheist, so long as he provokes no breach of the peace, may air his atheism as he pleases. The same is the case with the Press. A *Daily Herald* is as free to preach Socialism as *The Times* to preach Conservatism; and a Wells may, year by year, publish Utopias in which, greatly as each may differ from its predecessor, our present social order is always, directly or implicitly, assailed with considerable vigour.

Not one of these privileges would he be allowed for a day under Hitler, Mussolini, or Salazar. So far from protecting him, the police would arrest him, beat him, hurry him off to a prison, and try him—if it suited them to do so—when they chose, in secret or in public as they preferred. What would happen to him in prison may be guessed—for there would be no inspection; the prison is a dark place, and the dark places of the earth are full of cruelty. If the horrors became too great for bearing, and he sought refuge in death, even that would not be known to his friends: he would be " shot while attempting to escape ".

He might be a little more fortunate. He might have a chance of seeing the beauties of St. Kilda or Skye—which would lose some of their attractions after five years during which it was impossible to leave them; for gunboats would be constantly circling round.

As for the editors of papers—even of those which are now celebrating the achievements of the Hitlers and Kemals—they would find their liberties sadly circumscribed. They have now the *right* to tell the truth, whether they wish to exercise it or not. So soon as they were denied the right, they would become restive; and at the first sign of recalcitrance; the paper would be suppressed. They might hear of a piece of news—they would have to apply for permission before they could print it. It is by no means improbable—as I have hinted above—that among the first victims of Fascism would be the very men who, when it was at a distance, belauded its virtues. Nay, they might, in accordance with a Fascist principle, be punished retrospectively, with or without a trial, for a " crime " which was committed before the régime began, and which, under the old system, was not a crime at all. Nor, as these things may be done in secret, might their relatives ever receive the slightest information as to their fate.*

These privileges, which we enjoy, and of which the sub-

---

* Thus Mrs. Eggert was long in ignorance as to what had happened to her husband, who was shipped off from Brazil to Germany some months ago.

jects of a despotism are deprived, are so commonplace with us that we assume them as natural; they are like the air we breathe. It is therefore all the more necessary that we should make the effort of imagination, and try to picture what we should feel if we were to lose them. It should never be forgotten that they *are* privileges, in the full sense of the word—rights peculiar to special classes of people, and possessed by few nations. They have been won with pain and peril: and, like the riches of the children of those men who have acquired their wealth with infinite labour, they are too often held as matters of course, and may too easily be recklessly squandered. But the *duties* are even more worth retaining than the rights. The free citizen is under a moral compulsion. He is called upon, when exercising his free vote or his other free public functions, to weigh interests not his own; to be guided by another rule than his personal interests. He drops his ballot-paper into the box as one of a society, and of a society bound together not by force but by a common purpose. He is not a private in an army, driven on by a drill-sergeant; he is a willing partner in a great enterprise. This is the true public spirit, gained by intelligent study of opposing points of view *freely* presented to him, and not the sham one, forced upon him by the dictation of a single theory, the opportunity of considering others being denied. The moral effect of such an atmosphere of open discussion cannot be over-rated. It is true that its results are as yet very imperfectly attained; but we can see some shadow of what may be from the immense advance in popular intelligence since the enlargement of the franchise. Thousands, it must be confessed, still vote like sheep; " nourishing a blind life within the brain "; but thousands more, within the limits imposed by their chances, are studying, thinking, and deliberately choosing: and we may hope that the number of the thinkers will increase.*

But, on the other hand, it is necessary, if our Parliamentary system is to keep the confidence of the people, that it should be made truly popular. Much of the dissatisfaction which has recently been felt, and increasingly felt, with our institutions, is due to the fact that they are incompletely democratic. While everybody in the country over twenty-one has a vote, millions remain practically disfranchised, and are justly discontented in consequence. These, in the main, are Liberals, who, by the methods of reckoning their suffrages now in vogue, have no means of showing their real strength at the polls. A Liberal of the Right, disliking Socialism more than Toryism, is impelled to vote Conservative; and his vote is used to pass measures he detests. A Liberal of the Left, disliking Toryism more than Socialism, votes Labour, and again runs the risk of aiding policies which he thinks disastrous. Or, again, he may, in despair, abstain from voting, and his influence is utterly lost. If, *mirabile dictu*, he has a Liberal candidate to vote for, he but helps to put in one or other of the candidates with whom he disagrees. We thus find, repeatedly,

---

* I recall here the words of a man I know well, who has devoted fifty years to public service, as County Councillor, Mayor, and magistrate. He has, I should imagine, been as badly battered in debate, as vigorously abused, and as often defeated, as any man in England. He has seen his most sagacious plans obstructed, cut down, and, if finally passed, passed in debilitated shape. "Yet," said he, "I remain convinced that this is the best form of Government. Those obstructionists have been slowly learning how to govern. And," he added with a smile, "*sometimes* they have been right and I have been wrong."

a Government in power which does not in the least represent the dominant feeling in the country : and even the votes thus obtained, thousands of which simply mean that a *pis-aller* has been reluctantly chosen, are so badly distributed that, though on the showing of the votes themselves (deceptive as they are) the country is fairly evenly divided, one party gains a preposterously large Parliamentary majority. More than once, in the past, as in 1874 and in 1886, the votes have gone one way and the majority another ; and to-day, when the votes were 54 to 46, the proportion in the House of Commons was 44 to 19 : and the Liberals, who are probably about a quarter in the constituencies, are a negligible thirtieth in Parliament.* This is a serious defect in our system ; it is idle to speak of democracy in such circumstances ; and if our rulers wish that Parliament should be respected, they must alter it. It is of the essence of true democracy that minorities have rights. As things are, the minorities have hardly any political rights at all. Make a thing worth keeping, and as a rule people will desire to keep it. At present, the flaws in our institutions considerably diminish both their worth and the desire to keep them. They can, however, be mended without a revolution ; and, if they are mended, a revolution will be unlikely to come.

Another reform is easier to attain. Let the machinery of Parliament be speeded up. The waste of time is deplorable, unnecessary, and provocative of just resentment. To

* The system in America is still worse. If, in the State of New York, a party should gain a majority by a single vote, *all* the forty-seven votes in the Electoral college go to the candidate of the victorious party. Thus President Roosevelt, in the recent election, had a popular suffrage of about three to two. In the College his majority is 523 to 8.

take one example. The weary farce of divisions should be abolished. How many days of Parliamentary time are spent in this stupid perambulation every year would be hard to calculate; but it is certain that many Bills could be passed, in the days that might be saved, which are now periodically counted among the "slaughtered innocents". Here the Assembly of the State of Wisconsin, and probably those of many other States, are far in advance of the Mother of Parliaments. The Member records his vote, without leaving his seat, by touching a button. That vote is electrically recorded on an indicator, and the counting is done in a minute or two. Why our Members, who certainly in other respects show no disregard of their physical comfort, do not adopt some such device, is hard to understand.

But let the Constitution be never so democratic, and let its mechanical contrivances be never so perfect, something much more important yet remains. They must be worked in a sympathetic spirit; and the ruled must feel that the rulers do not rule over them but with them and for them. During, and for long after, the Napoleonic Wars the ministers and magistrates never tired of telling the people that the freedom of England was the envy and admiration of the world—and then sentenced their victims to transportation for a mild political speech or to hanging for stealing five shillings' worth of goods from a shop. We were, they announced, so free that we must not be permitted to ask for more freedom; we were so free that it was next door to treason to petition for a Ten-Hours' Day. The country, said Braxfield, belongs to the landed interest; and your liberty consists in doing what the "squire and his relations" bid you do. Something of this spirit still remains; and while much of it has vanished from our politics and legislation, it is still flagrant in our social life. There were, in 1914, working-men who, brought up on memories of the Hungry Forties, declared that there was no point in their fighting Germany; they would be no worse off under the Kaiser than under King George. They were wrong; but the causes that made them think so must not be allowed to occur. Such feelings arise less from actual want, or from jealousy of one's " betters ", than from the sight of insolence, contempt, or indifference in people more fortunately placed. It is here, more than anywhere else, that we need a change of heart.

It was a wise saying of John Richard Green's that even when the reality of freedom is destroyed, it is something to retain its forms. The liberties of England owe much to the fact that the tyranny of Thomas Cromwell was exercised through Parliament. When the tyranny was relaxed, Parliament was still there to resume, under happier auspices, the task of defending our people against prerogative. And Wordsworth, when one of the " Two Voices " of liberty had been silenced, cried to her :

" Of one deep bliss thine ear hath been bereft ;
  Then cleave, O cleave to that which still is left."

We have not lost our liberties; we have not yet fully attained them. But those we have, and the forms in which they are enshrined, are still elastic, and admit, without revolution, of being enlarged until there shall be none who do not feel themselves free men. As, in 1832, the middle classes gained, from Parliament, admission to Parliament, and thus peacefully acquired what France could win only by bloodshed and terror ; as later, Parliament deliberately threw open its doors wider and wider ; so, without upheavals, and by perfectly constitutional means, those who are still oppressed may gain what they need, and lose nothing in the process. Let them cleave to what they have, and thus be in a position to demand, and receive, more. If, in a fit of impatience or indignation, they endeavour to overthrow the work of ages, they may prove architects of ruin, and be overwhelmed beneath the falling walls.

APPENDIX

EVENTS move so fast that it is difficult even for reporters to keep up with them. One of the latest is Dr. Goebbels' instruction forbidding the criticism of works of art. Commentators are now forbidden to say whether such a work is good or bad, and must not write on it at all without eulogising the cultural and racial splendour of National Socialism. Hitherto, criticism has been tainted with Judaism and Liberalism; that must cease. Nor must anyone criticise a work unless he can himself do better than the artist he is appraising. "It cannot," said Goebbels, " be tolerated that, while in everything else the Führer's great constructive work was supported by public opinion, artists, of all people, should be the last victims of free criticism."

Earlier in the year (1936) Goebbels ordered dramatic and musical critics not to publish criticisms of evening performances before noon on the following day.

One may remember that, according to some, Juvenal was banished for criticising an actor.

INDEX

In this Index some Latin sentences are translated, and certain other phrases explained. The references are to pages: a subjoined *n* means a note on the page referred to; *sq* means that the subject is continued beyond the page indicated.

Abimelech, 23 *sq*, 131
Abyssinia, 17 *n*, 163
Achradina—outer part of Syracuse, 61
Adrastus—hero, worshipped, 37 *sq*
Aegean—sea, Archipelago, 51
Aeschylus—great Greek dramatist, 48
Aesymnete—Greek dictator, not tyrant, 15 *u*, 188
Aetna—Sicilian city, 60
Agariste, 41
Agathocles, 16, 69 *sq*., 96 (compared with Oliverotto by Machiavelli), the Younger, 75
Agrigentum—Sicilian city, 14, 55 *sq*., besieged by Carthaginians, 65
Albigenses—heretics of Provence, 140
Alcibiades—Olympic victor, 39
Alcmeonids—Athenian clan, 41, 49
Alexander—of Pherae, 32, 51
 the Great, 74
 the First, of Russia, 130
 the Second, of Russia, 207
 the Sixth, Pope, Rodrigo Borgia, 93
Alonso—Mariano, 117
Amasis—King of Egypt, abandoned Polycrates because he was too fortunate, 50
America—Southern States of, 54
Amiens—Peace of, 106
Anacreon—Greek poet, 51
Antander, 70
Apollo, 51

Archagathus, 75
"Architects of ruin"—phrase applied by Burke to French Revolutionaries, 127, 219
Areopagus—most venerable of Athenian courts, 47, "Mars' Hill."
Argos, 14, 37
"*Argumentum ad hominen*"—reasoning not general, but meant to suit the man you are arguing with; often sophistical, 131
Argyropoulos—Greek scholar, 86
Aricia—place where Diana was worshipped, 111
Arion—Greek poet, in story said to have been saved by a dolphin, 42
Ariosto—great Italian poet, 78
Aristides—"the Just", a man voted for his banishment because he was tired of always hearing him so called, 178
Aristodemus—tyrant of Cumae, 46 *n*
Aristogeiton—see Harmodius, 9
Aristotle—on tyranny, 8, 40 *n*, 42: on Dionysius, 63; his "Magnificent and Magnanimous Men," 82
"Aryans"—German fancy about, 178
Ascham—Roger, 87
Asuncion—chief city of Paraguay, 112, 114
Athaliah, 25
Athene—goddess of Athens, 17, 45

223

INDEX

Athens—"tyrant-city," 12, 14, 50
Augustus, 43
"*Ausi omnes immane nefas*"—title-page. "All dared a monstrous crime, and gained what they had dared", Virgil on tyrants.
Austria—gained territory by political lucky marriages, 41, see *Seipel* and *Dollfuss*

Bacchiads—Corinthian clan, 42
Bacon—Francis, on Charles VIII's expedition, 91
Barbour—his *Bruce* quoted, 209
Barras—chief of Directory, 101
Berthier—Napoleon's Chief of the Staff, 104
Bethel, 39
Bismarck, 168, 174
Blackshirts—Fascists, 146 sq., 151
Bolivar—chief general in delivering South America from Spain, 114
Bolsheviks, 140 sq.
Bomilcar—Carthaginian general, 74 sq.
Bonaparte—Lucien, 104, see *Napoleon*
Borgia—see *Alexander VI*. Caesar, 93 sq.; Lucretia, 94; Giovanni (Duke of Gandia), 94
Braunau—(*au* as *how*) Hitler's birthplace, 170
Braxfield—notorious Scottish judge (original of Stevenson's *Weir of Hermiston*), 217
Brazen Bull—of Phalaris; victims thrown into it, and a fire kindled below; their cries came out as the roaring of the bull, 20, 56
Brazil, 121 sq.
Brumaire—French Republican month, nearly = November. On the 18th, 1799, a revolution made Napoleon practically ruler of France, 104
Bruttians—a people in the south-west of Italy, 70
Brutus—murderer of Julius Caesar, 148
Buckingham—Duke of, supported Richard III, and later quarrelled with him, 20

Caballero, 126
Cadoudal, 107
"*Caelum non animum*"—a line of Horace, "they change their sky but not their mind who cross the sea", 51
Caesar—Julius, 13, 30, 137, 187, see *Borgia*
Caligula—mad Roman Emperor, 130
Cambyses—King of Persia, 11 130
Canossa—here the Emperor Henry IV made a humiliating surrender to Pope Gregory VII. "To go to Canossa" is a proverb for such a submission. During a quarrel with the Papacy Bismarck said he would not go to Canossa; but he had to go half-way, 183
Caporetto—Italian defeat, 146
Carcinus, 70
Carlyle—on Francia, 111 sq.
Carmona—military ruler of Portugal, 137
Carro Leon, 126
Carthage, 53 sq.; see *Sicily*
Catalonia, 166
Catana—city of Sicily, 60
Cavour—Italian statesman of the fifties, 99, 144
Caxias—Brazilian general, 125
Chaco, 122
Chalcondylas—scholar, 86
Chamberlain—H. Stewart, 171
Charles—I, of England, 7; V, Emperor, 83, 93; VIII, of France, 90 sq.
Chaucer—quoted, 47
China, 15 n

INDEX

Chouans—Royalists of Britanny, 105
Christian—mad king of Denmark, 130
Chromius—Nemean Victor, 40
Cicero—on tyrants, 8, 13, 32 : 62
Cincinnatus—Roman dictator, 16
Cirrha—Greek city, 40
Cleisthenes—of Sicyon, 37 *sq.*
Cleomenes—Spartan king, 48
Clement VII—Giulio de' Medici, 83, 92
Cleon—Athenian demagogue, 12
Coinage—influence on tyranny, 27, 35
Coleridge—quoted, 135 *n*, 200
Colonna—great Roman family, 55
Corcyra—Corfu, 43
Corinth, 9, 35 ; see *Periander*
Corrientes, 123
Cromwell—Oliver, 7, 35, 106, 135, 187 ; Thomas, 79, 218
Cremona, 151
Crotona—Greek city in South Italy, 70
Cumae, 46 *n*, 60
Cypselus—tyrant of Corinth, 42
Cyrene, 74

Damocles, 63 ; the sword which Dionysius hung over his head by a thread is proverbial.
Damon and Phintias—(or Pythias), 63
Darius—King of Persia, 49
David, 32
De Bono—Italian general in Abyssinian war, 17 *n*, 155 *sq.*
Delphi—seat of Apollo's oracle, 40, 64
Demos—the people as distinct from the aristocracy, 54, 58, etc.
D'Eu—Comte, Brazilian general, 126
Dictator—inexact name, 15 *sq.*
Dimitroff—Communist, 177
Dionysius—the Elder, tyrant of Syracuse, 21, 28, 61 *sq.* ; his son, the Younger, 69, 70

Directory—French government after the Terror, 101
" *Divide et impera* "—Divide and conquer ; Roman maxim as to dealing with enemies, 146
Dollfuss, 188 *sq.*
" *Dolce far niente* "—" Sweet do-nothing ", 115
Donation of Constantine—an imaginary gift of Constantine the Great to Pope Sylvester ; on which the Temporal Power of the Popes was supposed to be based, 161
Dorieus—of Rhodes —(*eu* as *ew* in *news*), 39
Drake—Sir Francis, 53
Dual Monarchy—In 1867 Austria and Hungary were separated, and became entirely independent ; but the Emperor of Austria and the King of Hungary were always to be the same person. It was like the relation of England and Scotland under the Stuarts, 188
Duce—(Du-chay), Leader, title of Mussolini, 158, etc.
Ducos—the Third Consul in the first Consulate of Napoleon, 104
Dumini—murderer of Matteotti, 156

East India Company—Carthage compared to, 53
Ecclesiastes—quoted, 7 ; " There is nothing new under the sun, neither can anyone say, Lo, this hath not been before."
Egesta—Sicel city of Sicily, 75
Eggert—Luci, fate of her husband, 213 *n*
El-Berith—" God of Covenant ", 31
Eliphaz—his speech in *Job*, quoted, 10
Elis—in N.W. of Morea, 36

INDEX

Enghien—(*i* silent), Duke of, shot by Napoleon, 108
Ersatz—(*s* as *z*), substitute; familiar word during the War for German substitute-foods, etc.
Este—ruling family in Ferrara, 78
  Niccolo, 85
  Leonello, 85
Eteocles—king of Thebes, character in play of Euripides, 13
Eubœa—the Negropont, its talent, 36
Euripides—Athenian dramatist, quoted, 13, 34

Fabius—Cunctator, the "Dawdler," Roman dictator, 16
Facta—Italian Prime Minister, 150 *sq.*
Fascists—19, 147 *sq.*
  (pronounced Fashists)
Ferro—on Salazar, 137 *n*
Fey—Major, Austrian soldier, 195 *sq.*
Filelfo—Renaissance scholar, 88
Finland—annexed to Russia, 139
Florence—80 *sq.*; see Medici
Fogliano—murdered by Oliverotto, 95
Forni—semi-Fascist, 154
Fouché—Napoleon's police-minister, 105
Francia—Rodriguez, Dictator of Paraguay, 111 *sq.*, 163
Franco—Spanish general, 16, 166
Frederick William—of Prussia, 119
Frederick II—"the Great", 121
Führer—"Leader", Hitler's title, 17, 181, etc.
Fulgencio—shot by Francia, 112 *sq.*

Gaal—30 *sq.*
Galeotae—Sicilian interpreters of omens, 63

Gandia—Duke of, 94
Garibaldi—144
Garigliano—battle, 91
Gela—city of Sicily, 56
Gelo—tyrant of Syracuse, 56 *sq.*
Gerizim—mountain, 28
George III—130
Gideon—=Jerubbaal, 25 *sq.*
Goebbels—134, 175, Appendix
Goethe—on patriotism, 168
Goldsmith—quoted, 168 *u*
Gombos, 196
Gonfaloniere—"standard-bearer", title of chief officer in Florence, 80
Gonzaga—rulers of Mantua, 86 *sq.*
Göring, 176
Green—J. R., historian, 218
Gregory—J. D., *Life of Dollfuss*, 188 *n*
Grey—Lady Jane, 87
Guarino—scholar, 85, 87
Gulliver, 191.

Hamilcar—Carthaginian general, 71
Hannibal—son of Gisco, conquered Himera, 65; the great son of Hamilcar Barca, his ring, 76
Hanno, 74
Harmodius—and Aristogeiton, 9, 48
Hawkins—seaman, 53
Hebrew tyrants, 23 *sq.*
Hegel—German philosopher, 181
Heimwehr, 191
Henry VIII, 83
Heracles—Greek name for Hercules, 35
Hegemony—overlordship, falling short of direct rule, 205
Hermeias—Greek tyrant, 9
Hermocrates—father of Dionysius, 62; son of Hermon, 64 *sq.*
Herodotus—Greek historian, quoted, 11, 41, 47, 50, 58, 209

INDEX

Hiero—of Syracuse, 39, 59 *sq.*
Himera—Sicilian city, 59
Himilco—Carthaginian general, 65
Hindenburg, 170, 173
Hipparchus, 48, 51
Hippias, 48 *sq.*
Hippocleides, 41
Hippocrates, 57
Hitler—Adolf, 16, 17, 170 *sq.*, 192
Hoche—Lazare, French Republican general, 103
Hoare—Sir Samuel, 167
Hohenlinden—battle, 105
Holy Alliance—after Waterloo, between Austria, Prussia, and Russia, 201
Homer, 35
Horace, 43
Hortensius—his law which made Rome a democracy, 201
Hugenberg, 180
Humphrey—Duke of Gloucester, a lover of learning, 86
Hungry Forties—the period about 1840 when the poor suffered from semi-starvation, 218

"*Index expurgatorius*"—properly a list of books drawn up by Catholic authorities declaring which may be read after being expurgated. There is also an Index of entirely prohibited books. Both phrases are often used in a loose or general sense, 196
Iraq—a country of Mesopotamia, 100
Israel, 23 *sq.*

"Jacob Omnium"—Matthew Higgins, who is said to have begun the practice of writing letters to newspapers, 210
Jehu, 24

Jeroboam, 23 *sq.*
Jerubbaal—Gideon, 32, 39
Jews—in Germany, 177 *sq.*
Johnson—Dr., quoted, 152; 203
Josephus—Jewish historian, quoted, 23
Jotham, 32
Julius II—Pope, 97
Juvenal—Latin poet, on the ring in which Hannibal kept poison, with which he at last killed himself, and which was the vindex or avenger of his victims, 76; quoted, 8; "*Sic volo*"—"so I will, so I command, let caprice stand instead of reason."

Karl—Austrian Emperor, 189
Karl-Marx-Hof — workmen's buildings in Vienna, 124
Kemal—Mustapha, ruler of Turkey since the War, 100, 201
Koebel—author of an account of Paraguay, 124
Kienbock—Austrian politician, 192

Laberius—Roman knight, compelled by Julius Caesar to the indignity of acting in his own play. He retorted by reciting some lines, of which one is, "Needs must he whom many fear, fear many", 50, 63
Lampedusa—Mediterranean island, prison for Italian Liberals, 160
Lannes—Marshal, when mortally wounded urged Napoleon to give up war, 110
League of Nations, 207, etc.
Lenin, 140 *sq.*, 145
Leo X—Pope, Giovanni de' Medici, 92
Leonardo—da Vinci, 78
Leontini—Sicilian city, 63, 67

INDEX

Lipari—islands north of Sicily, used as prisons for Italian Liberals, 160

Locri—Greek city in South Italy, 61

Lopez—Don Carlos Antonio, ruler of Paraguay, 117 sq.; Don Francisco, his son, Dictator, 119 sq.

Louis XII—of France, 91, 97

Lucretius—great Latin poet, quoted, 78; "From the midst of a fountain of sweets there rises something bitter."

Ludendorff—German general, 171

Lutheran Church—always closely allied with the State, 181

Lycurgus—legendary founder of Spartan system, alluded to, 36; head of an Athenian clan, 44 sq.

Lygdamis—tyrant of the Aegean island of Naxos, 46

Lynch—Madame, associated with Francisco Lopez, 120, 126

Macbeth—play quoted, 55

Machiavelli, 69, 79, 94, 96 sq., quoted, 100, 159

Madeira, 137 n, 160

Maecenas—Minister of Augustus, proverbial patron of literature, 84

Maenon—murders Agathocles, 76

Magians—Persian usurpers, 11

Magna Graccia—Greater Greece, Southern Italy, 51, 52

"*Magni nominis umbra*"—phrase used by the poet Lucan of Pompey, when he was no longer the man he was; "shadow of a great name", 170

Majorca, 205

Mantua, 86

Marathon—Persian defeat, 50

Maret—French diplomatist, 105

Marlowe—his "Tamburlaine", 79

Marsilio Ficino—scholar, 84

Marten—Henry, Republican of Charles I's time, quoted, 131

Massena—great French general, 101

Masterman—Englishman in Paraguay, 121

Matteotti—murdered by Fascists, 155 sq., 197

Mazzini—(z as ts) Italian Republican, 9 u.

Medici—Florentine family:
Cosimo, 79 sq.
Giovanni (father), 80
Piero (elder), 81
Lorenzo—the Magnificent, 81 sq.
Giuliano, 82 (*gi* nearly = *j*)
Giovanni—Leo X, 92
Giulio—Clement VII, 83, 92
Lorenzo—the Younger, 92
Catherine—Queen of Henry II of France, 92
Alessandro, 92
Lorenzino, 92, 93
Cosimo—first Duke of Florence, 93

"*Medio de fonte*"—see *Lucretius*, 78

Megacles, 41 sq.

Megara—in Greece Proper, 51, 57; in Sicily, 57

Melanippus—Theban hero, 38

Metaxas—despot of modern Greece, 137

Michael Angelo, 78, 84

Miklas—Austrian President, 191

Milan, 87, 98

Miletus, 51

Mill—John Stuart, 207 sq.

Milton—on Education, 89

Minos—King of Crete, 51

Mitre—Argentine general, 125

Mitylene—see *Pittacus*, 15 n

Monophysites—Christians who believe that Christ has only one nature: the Abyssinian Church holds this creed, 164

INDEX

Moreau—French Republican general, 103, 105, 107 sq.
Mosley—Oswald, 212
Mowrer—journalist, his *Germany Puts the Clock Back*, 173
Muller—Bishop supporting Hitler, 182
Mussolini, 16, 146, sq., 192

Nabis—Spartan tyrant, 76
Nantes—Revocation of Edict of, 160
Naples, 161; kingdom of, 98
Napoleon—the Great, on Wellington, 15 n; and the Press, 37; quoted, 56; 75, 100 sq., 160, 167, 187. Napoleon III, 47, 69, 106, 132
Naxos—island in the Aegean, 46
Nazis—171 sq. (National Socialists)
" Necesse est " etc.—see Laberius
Nemean Games—40
Nemesis—the goddess or principle which punishes arrogance or excessive good-fortune, 50
Nestor—oldest Greek hero at Troy, 26
Niemoller—Protestant German pastor, 182
Nordics, 171
Novi—battle in Italy in which the French were defeated and General Joubert killed, 102

Oates—Titus, 176, 197
Oligarchies—rule of the rich few, 61, etc.
Oliverotto—da Fermo, 95
Olympic Games, 39, etc.
Ophellas—Greek general, 74
Orlando—Italian Prime Minister, 144, 153
Orsini—great Roman family, 55
Orthagoras—founder of tyrant-dynasty in Sicyon, 37
Ortygia—inner part of Syracuse, 61, 68

Otanes—Persian noble; imaginary speech of, 11, 33

Padua, 86
Palacio—Bishop, 121
Palermo—(Panormus) 59
Palmerston—English Premier, 161 n
Pan-hellenic—concerning the whole of Greece, 77
Papen, 174
Paraguay, 111 sq.
Patmore—Coventry, poet, quoted, 202
Paul—Russian Czar, 130
Pazzi—Florentine family, 83
Peisistratus—17, 43 sq.
Perez—his sermon on Francia, 115
Periander—of Corinth, 42 sq.
Pericles, 12, 79
Persians, 11, 12, 49
Phalaris—of Agrigentum, 20, 55 sq., 131
Phaonius—his remark to Brutus, 148
Pheidon—of Argos, 14, 21, 27, 34 sq.
Philip—of Macedon, 40 n, 62
Philistus—historian, 62
Phœnissae—" Phœnician Women," play of Euripides, 13
Phrynichus—dramatist, 48
Pichegru—French general, 107 sq.
Pilsudski—ruler of Poland, 16, 132 n
Pindar—great lyric poet, 39, 64
Pittacus—of Mitylene, 15 n, 188
Pitti—Luca, his conspiracy, 81
Pius II—Pope (Aeneas Sylvius), 86: very learned
Plataea—city in Greece, near Thebes, 57
Plato, 10, 64; his works translated by Ficino, 84
Plutarch, 20, 100
Poggio—Bracciolini, scholar, 86
Pole—Reginald, Cardinal, 79
Polignac—extreme Royalist, 107

INDEX

Politian—scholar, 84
Polycrates—tyrant of Samos, 50
Polyzelus, 60
Primo de Rivera—ruler of Spain, 166
" Prince "—by Machiavelli, rules for despots, 79, 97
Pulci—Italian poet, 85
Pythian Games—at Delphi, in honour of Apollo, 40

Quintilian—great Roman teacher of rhetoric ; discovery of some of his books by Poggio, 86

Regulus—invaded Carthage, 73
Reichstag—German Imperial Parliament, fire at, 178
Renaissance, 78 sq.
Revolution—French, 100 sq. 141 sq.
Rheneia—small island near Samos, 51.
Richard II, 35
Richard III—28 ; play quoted, 24 n
Rintelen, 194 sq.
Romagna—(gn like ny) district of Italy, 95
Roosevelt—President, 216 n.
Rosenberg, 182
Rovere—Cardinal delle, Pope Julius II, 97

Sacred War, 40
St. Germain—Peace of, 188
Salamis—battle, 59
Salandra—Italian Prime Minister, 153
Salazar—Oliveira, ruler of Portugal, 21, 132
Salvemini—Italian professor, exiled, 159
Samos—Aegean island, 50, 51, 57

Samuel—Book of, 32
" Saturnian Age "—an age in which Italy, ruled by the god Saturn, was supposed to have had perfect happiness, 143
Saul, 32
Savonarola—great religious reformer of Florence, 91
Schleicher—murdered by Nazis, 181
Scholars—honoured by tyrants in Renaissance age, 85 sq.
Schuschnigg, 191 sq.
Seipel—Monsignor, Premier of Austria, 189 sq.
Seitz—Socialist Mayor of Vienna, 190
Sennacherib—King of Assyria, 68
Seven Against Thebes—legendary war before the war of Troy, 37
Seven Wise Men of Greece, 15 n, 44
Seven Years' War—the war in which Quebec was taken, 168
Sforza—Milanese family ; Lodovico calls in French, 90
Shechem, 29 sq.
Sicily, 52 sq.
" Sic volo, sic jubeo "—see Juvenal
Sicyon—Greek city in Morea, 14, 37
Sieyès—Abbé (final s sounded), 102 sq.
Sigeum—town not far from Troy, 49
Simonides—Greek poet, 40, 60
Sinigaglia—Italian town, 96
Sixtus IV—Pope, 83, 84 .
Smyrna—city of Asia Minor, 143
Sobieski—John, King of Poland, who in 1683 saved Vienna from the Turks, 191
Solomon, 44, 47
Solon—great Athenian statesman, 44 sq.
Sosicles—Corinthian speaker, 49

INDEX

Sparta—long the leading city in Greece 13, 48 *sq.* ; later, under tyranny of Nabis, 76

Spinoza—great philosopher of the seventeenth century, 79

Stalin—ruler of Soviet Russia, 143, 154

Starhemberg—Austrian statesman, 191 *sq.*

Streicher—leader of anti-Jewish propaganda, 179

Stresemann—Foreign Minister of Germany before rise of Hitler, 170

Sulla—great Roman Dictator, 16

Sybel—German historian of the French Revolution, 187

Syracuse—chief city of Sicily, 14, 56 *sq.*, 62 *sq.*

Tacitus—on Tiberius, 10 ; his *Annals* discovered by Poggio, 86 ; (*c* soft)

Talleyrand, 105

Tarquin—the Proud, tyrannical king of Rome, 43, 46 *n*, 117

Terillus—tyrant of Himera, 59

Tevego—place of exile in Paraguay, 115

Thalassocrats—rulers of the sea, 51

Theagenes—of Megara, 51

Thebans, 57

Thebez, 32

Theron—of Agrigentum, 39

Thespis—traditional founder of Athenian tragedy, 48

Third Estate—tiers Etat, the middle classes of France, 103

Thompson—English visitor to Paraguay, 121, 124 *sq.*

Thrasybulus—of Miletus, 51 ; of Syracuse, 61

Thucydides—Greek historian 27, 47, 51, 79

Tiberius—Roman Emperor, his letter to the Senate, 10

Timoleon—Corinthian enemy of tyranny, 9, 70

Tiptoft—John, Earl of Worcester, 86

"Tite Barnacle"—Dickens's type of the arrogant Civil Servant, 211

Torgler—German Communist, 177

Toscanini, 159

Tripoli, 164

Ukraine—in Russia, 172

Urbino—taken by Caesar Borgia, 95

Uriah the Hittite, 32

Uruguay, 123 *sq.*

Valentinois—Caesar Borgia, duke of, 97

Valery—Paul, on Salazar, 132

Venezuela, 122

Venice, 87

Virgil—quoted, 42 *u* ; "Begin, O child, to recognise thy mother with a smile", 43

Vitelli, 95

Vittorino da Feltre, 86 *sq.*

Voltaire—his quarrel with Frederick the Great, 64

Wal-wal, 163

William the Conqueror, 55

Wilson—President of the United States, 144, 200

Woodward—W. H., his *Life of Vittorino*, 87

Wordsworth—quoted, 218

Xerxes, 47

Zamboni, 197

Zebul, 30

Zollverein (*z* as *ts*, *v* as *f*, *ei* as *i* in *fine*) customs-union ; a system of free-trade among the German States, established by Bismarck, 188

Zoroaster, 42 *n*